To the Reader:

Scientology® religious philosophy contains pastoral counseling procedures intended to assist an individual to gain greater knowledge of self. The mission of the Church of Scientology is a simple one: to help the individual achieve greater self-confidence and personal integrity, thereby enabling him to really trust and respect himself and his fellow man. The attainment of the benefits and goals of Scientology philosophy requires each individual's dedicated participation, as only through his own efforts can he achieve these.

This book is based on the religious literature and works of the Scientology Founder, L. Ron Hubbard. It is presented to the reader as part of the record of his personal research into life, and the application of same by others, and should be construed only as a written report of such research and not as a statement of claims made by the Church or the Founder.

Scientology philosophy and its forerunner, Dianetics® technology, as practiced by the Church, address only the "thetan" (spirit). Although the Church, as are all churches, is free to engage in spiritual healing, it does not, as its primary goal is increased spiritual awareness for all. For this reason, the Church does not wish to accept individuals who desire treatment of physical or mental illness but prefers to refer these to qualified specialists of other organizations who deal in these matters.

The Hubbard® Electrometer is a religious artifact in the Church Confessional. It in itself does nothing, and is used by ministers only to assist parishioners in locating areas of spiritual distress or travail.

We hope the reading of this book is only the first stage of a personal voyage of discovery into this new and vital world religion.

This Book Belongs to:

_____

_____
(Date)

Church of Scientology International

SCIENTOLOGY
The Fundamentals of Thought

L. RON HUBBARD

SCIENTOLOGY
The Fundamentals of Thought

Bridge
PUBLICATIONS, INC.

Published in the U.S.A. by
Bridge Publications, Inc.
4751 Fountain Avenue
Los Angeles, California 90029

ISBN 0-88404-341-X

Published in other countries by
New Era® Publications International, ApS
Store Kongensgade 55
1264 Copenhagen K, Denmark

ISBN 87-7336-581-5

Printed in the United States of America

Important Note

In reading this book, be very certain you never go past a word you do not fully understand.

The only reason a person gives up a study or becomes confused or unable to learn is because he or she has gone past a word that was not understood.

The confusion or inability to grasp or learn comes AFTER a word that the person did not have defined and understood.

Have you ever had the experience of coming to the end of a page and realizing you didn't know what you had read? Well, somewhere earlier on that page you went past a word that you had no definition for or an incorrect definition for.

Here's an example. "It was found that when the crepuscule arrived the children were quieter and when it was not present, they were much livelier." You see what happens. You think you don't understand the whole idea, but the inability to understand came entirely from the one word you could not define, *crepuscule*, which means twilight or darkness.

It may not only be the new and unusual words that you will

have to look up. Some commonly used words can often be misdefined and so cause confusion.

This datum about not going past an undefined word is the most important fact in the whole subject of study. Every subject you have taken up and abandoned had its words which you failed to get defined.

Therefore, in studying this book be very, very certain you never go past a word you do not fully understand. If the material becomes confusing or you can't seem to grasp it, there will be a word just earlier that you have not understood. Don't go any further, but go back to BEFORE you got into trouble, find the misunderstood word and get it defined.

Definitions

As an aid to the reader, words most likely to be misunderstood have been defined in footnotes the first time they occur in the text. Words sometimes have several meanings. The footnote definitions in this book only give the meaning that the word has as it is used in the text. Other definitions for the word can be found in a dictionary.

A glossary including all the footnote definitions is at the back of this book.

Table of Contents

Introduction

While *Scientology: The Fundamentals of Thought* was originally published as a résumé[1] of Scientology for use in transla-
tions into non-English tongues, the book itself is of inestimable
value to the beginner or advanced student of the mind and life.

Containing much material new to Scientologists, the book
forms a compact but broad survey of the subject.

Equipped with this book alone, the student of the mind
could begin a practice and perform seeming miracles in changing the states of health, ability and intelligence of people.

No such knowledge has ever before existed and no such
results have ever before been attainable by man as those which
can be reached by a study of this brief volume.

Give this book to a man or a woman in trouble, a man or
a woman with an inquiring nature, a man or a woman with

---

1. **résumé:** a summing up; summary.

associates who need a better life, and let that man or woman study this volume carefully and apply it. Change and a better life will result.

This book is a summation,[2] if brief, of the results of fifty thousand years of thinking men. Their materials, researched and capped by a quarter of a century of original search by L. Ron Hubbard, have brought the humanities,[3] so long outdistanced by the "exact sciences," into a state of equality, if not superiority, to physics,[4] chemistry[5] and mathematics.

What has been attempted by a thousand universities and foundations[6] at a cost of billions has been completed quietly here.

This *is* how life works. This *is* how you change men and women and children for the better.

The use or neglect of this material may well determine the use or neglect of the atomic bomb by man. Scientology is already winning in this field. In the same period in history, two of the most sweeping forces man has known have come to fruition:[7] a knowledge of himself and others with Scientology, and a means of destroying himself and all others by atomic fission. Which

---

2. **summation:** a work giving a summary of a whole subject.

3. **humanities:** the branches of learning concerned with human thought and relations, as distinguished from the sciences.

4. **physics:** the science dealing with the properties, changes and interactions, etc., of matter and energy.

5. **chemistry:** the science dealing with the composition and properties of substances, and with the reactions by which substances are produced from or converted into other substances.

6. **foundations:** institutions financed by a donation or legacy to aid research, education, the arts, etc.

7. **fruition:** a coming to fulfillment; realization.

force wins depends in a large measure on your use of Scientology.

Scientology is today, around the world, represented on every continent on Earth. As you read this, this very book is being translated into many non-English tongues and is being distributed to nations whose thronging multimillions have never before been touched by Anglo-American[8] thought.

As L. Ron Hubbard has said in an essay:

Scientology and Scientologists are not revolutionaries. They are evolutionaries.[9] They do not stand for overthrow. They stand for the improvement of what we have.

Scientology is not political. When the fires of ideology[10] threaten to consume us all, it is time to forget politics and seek reason.

The mission of Scientology is not conquest—it is civilization. It is a war upon stupidity, the stupidity which leads us toward the Last War of All.

To a Scientologist, the real barbarism of Earth is stupidity. Only in the black muck of ignorance can the irrational conflicts of ideologies germinate.[11]

Government, to a Scientologist, is a thing of reason and

---

8. **Anglo-American:** belonging to, relating to or involving England and America, especially the United States, or the people of the two countries.

9. **evolutionaries:** those concerned with evolution or development.

10. **ideology:** the principal ideas or beliefs that characterize a particular class, group or movement.

11. **germinate:** to start developing or growing.

all problems of government can be resolved by reason.

Perhaps in yesterday one could afford the exploita-tion[12] of ignorance for the sake of fancied gain. Perhaps in yesterday the study of the mind and reason was some-thing for a summer afternoon. Perhaps in that same yesterday one among us could afford his irresponsibility and hate.

But that was yesterday. Today, exploited ignorance, a dilettante[13] attitude toward existing knowledge, a re-fusal to assume one's role as a responsible member of the human race, may be punished in the searing thunder-clap of H-bombs released by men whose intelligence and statecraft[14] were incapable of a better solution. Ignorant people elect ignorant rulers. And only ignorant rulers lead to war—and this time will lead to a war which will bring silence forever after to Earth.

As your associates, their homes, their children, their possessions and all their future lie ending in a radioac-tive street, there won't be time for us to wish we'd worked harder, been less easily dissuaded[15] from press-ing our arguments. The copies of this book you did not distribute will lie there too.

Some say they have no fear of death until the midnight of their dying is at hand. They say different, then.

---

12. **exploitation:** making unethical use of for one's own advantage or profit.

13. **dilettante:** of or characteristic of a person who follows an art or science only for amusement and in a superficial way.

14. **statecraft:** the art of government and diplomacy.

15. **dissuaded:** turned aside (from a course, etc.) by persuasion or advice.

Those who strike at this work out of some black well of ideological misorientation,[16] some antisocial cravenness,[17] strike at the heart of man—for man has been a long time on the track to reason, and Scientology can take him there.

There is not much Earth time. We must work.

The criminal is ignorant and stupid. Ignorance and stupidity may therefore be called criminal.

Cause man to lay aside his hates and listen. Freedom from ignorance is at hand. Perhaps that was the Kingdom of Heaven.

There is not much Earth time in which to distribute this knowledge. This is the solution to our barbarism out of which we would lose all. Scientology works. We must work, all of us—not to harangue[18] man toward impossible freedoms, but to make man civilized enough to be worthy of his freedom.

It is time man grew up. That is what we have in mind. For there can be but weeping in the night where ignorance, factionalism,[19] hatred and exploitation are served by the most ferocious and final weapon of all—the H-bomb.

---

16. **misorientation:** wrong placing or positioning with regard to facts or principles.

17. **cravenness:** condition of being very cowardly or afraid.

18. **harangue:** to scold or address with a long or intense verbal attack.

19. **factionalism:** condition of conflict, discord or antagonism among members of a group.

Change no man's religion, change no man's politics, interrupt the sovereignty[20] of no nation. Instead, teach man to use what he has and what he knows to the factual creation, within any political reference, of a civilization on Earth for the first time.

And so we work.

We trust you will find this volume of use in your home life and your business. We hope that by placing it in your hands, you and many others can lead better lives.

—The Editors

Note: This text has been organized so that a complete translation of all of it will deliver, without interruption or destructive change, the basics of Scientology into non-English tongues.

---

20. **sovereignty:** supreme and independent power or authority in government as possessed or claimed by a state or community.

1

The
Vital Statistics
of Scientology

1

The Vital Statistics of Scientology

What is Scientology?

Scientology is an applied religious philosophy.

The term *Scientology* is taken from the Latin word *scio* (knowing in the fullest meaning of the word) and the Greek word *logos* (study of). In itself the word means literally "knowing how to know."

Scientology is further defined as the study and handling of the spirit in relationship to itself, universes and other life.

Any comparison between Scientology and the subject known as psychology is nonsense. Early psychology such as that begun by St. Thomas Aquinas[1] and extended by many later authors was, in 1879, interrupted severely by one Professor Wundt,[2] a Marxist[3] at Leipzig University in Germany. This man conceived that man was an animal without soul and based all of

---

1. **St. Thomas Aquinas:** (1225?–74) Italian religious philosopher.

2. **Wundt:** Wilhelm Wundt (1832–1920), German physiologist and psychologist.

3. **Marxist:** follower or believer in the doctrines of Karl Marx (1818–83), German political philosopher, regarded by some as the founder of modern socialism.

his work on the principle that there was no *psyche* (a Greek word meaning "spirit"). Psychology, the study of the spirit (or mind) then came into the peculiar position of being "a study of the spirit which denied the spirit." For the subsequent decades, Wundtian "psychology" was taught broadly throughout the world. It taught that man was an animal. It taught that man could not be bettered. It taught that intelligence never changed. This subject, Wundtian psychology, became standard, mainly because of the indifference or lack of knowledge of people in charge of universities.

Scientology can and does change behavior and intelligence, and it can and does assist people to study life. Unlike Wundtian pseudo-psychology, it has no political aspiration.[4] Scientology is not teaching dialectical materialism[5] under the heading of "psychology."

Scientology is a *route*, a way, rather than a dissertation[6] or an assertive[7] body of knowledge.

Through its drills and studies one may find the truth for oneself. It is the only thing that can show you who *you* really are.

---

4. **aspiration:** strong desire or ambition.

5. **dialectical materialism:** in logic, "dialectic" is the action and reaction between opposites, out of which a new synthesis (harmony of the two opposites) emerges. This was an idea originated by the German philosopher Georg Wilhelm Hegel (1770–1831). "Materialism" is a philosophy which falsely maintains that there is nothing in the universe but matter, that mind is a phenomenon of matter, and that there is no ground for assuming a spiritual first cause. "Dialectical materialism" was an adaptation of these ideas by German revolutionary leader and founder of modern socialism Karl Marx (1818–83) into his own "general laws of motion which govern the evolution of nature and society." He held that a conflict of opposites in human society is the evolutionary process by which a classless society would eventually be reached.

6. **dissertation:** a formal discussion of a subject.

7. **assertive:** confidently aggressive or self-assured.

The technology is therefore not expounded[8] as something to believe but something to *do*.

The end result of Scientology studies and drills is a renewed awareness of self as a spiritual and immortal[9] being.

Only those who believe, as do psychiatrists and psychologists, that man is a soulless animal or who wish for their own reasons to keep man unhappy and oppressed are in any conflict with Scientology.

Scientology, used by the trained and untrained person, improves the health, ability, intelligence, behavior, skill and appearance of people.

It is a precise and exact science, designed for an age of exact sciences.

It is employed by an *auditor*[10] upon individuals or small or large groups of people in their presence. The auditor makes these people, at their choice, do various exercises, and these exercises bring about changes for the better in intelligence, behavior and general competence.

Scientology is employed as well by business and government persons to solve problems and to establish better organization.

It is also employed by the average person to bring better order into life.

---

8. **expounded:** explained or interpreted.

9. **immortal:** not liable or subject to death; undying.

10. **auditor:** a person trained and qualified in applying Scientology procedures to individuals for their betterment; called an auditor because *auditor* means "one who listens."

How is Scientology used?

Scientology is employed by an auditor as a set of drills upon the individual, and small or large groups. It is also employed as an educational subject. It has been found that persons can be processed[11] in Scientology with Scientology exercises and can be freed from their major anxieties and can become brighter, more alert and more competent. *But* if they are *only* processed they have a tendency to be overwhelmed[12] or startled, and although they may be brighter and more competent they are still held down by an ignorance of life. Therefore it is far better to teach *and* process a person than only to process him. In other words, the best use of Scientology is through processing and education in Scientology. In this way there is no imbalance. It is interesting that people only need to study Scientology to have some small rise in their own intelligence, behavior and competence. The study itself is therapeutic by actual testing.

It is also used by business and government leaders to establish or improve organization.

It is used as well by the individual at home or at his work to make a better life.

Is Scientology valid?

Tens of thousands of case histories, all sworn to, are in the possession of the organizations of Scientology. No other subjects on Earth except physics and chemistry have had such grueling testing. Scientology in the hands of an expert can restore man's ability to handle any and all of his problems. Scientology is used

---

11. **processed:** have Scientology processes and procedures applied to someone by a trained practitioner. Also called "audited."

12. **overwhelmed:** overcome completely in mind or feeling.

by some of the largest companies on Earth. It is valid. It has been tested. It is the only thoroughly tested system of improving human relations, intelligence and character, and is the only one which does.

Where is there more information about Scientology?

There are Scientology organizations located throughout the world. Scientology practitioners[13] are validated by these organizations. Diplomas are given only after *very* exact training. A person who is skilled in Scientology procedures has a diploma from one of these organizations. A list of these organizations is provided at the back of this book.

These offices and these people can give you more information about Scientology.

There have also been many books published on the subjects of Dianetics[14] and Scientology. A full list of these books is given in the bibliography at the back of this volume.

Can a person without much study use Scientology?

Scientology is practiced in daily life by enormous numbers of people who have no formal training in the humanities beyond a study of textbooks. Scientology was developed to be used by such people as well as by the trained practitioner. A person studying by himself from textbooks can use Scientology to help his fellow human beings.

---

13. **practitioners:** persons engaged in the practice of a profession, occupation, etc.

14. **Dianetics:** man's most advanced school of the mind. The word comes from Greek *dia* (through) and *nous* (soul). Dianetics is defined as what the soul is doing to the body. It is a way of handling the energy of which life is made in such a way as to bring about a greater efficiency in the organism and in the spiritual life of the individual.

What special use does Scientology have?

Scientology does things for people where nothing has been done before. It restores people's ability to handle conditions which were once considered hopeless. It increases their intelligence. It changes their competence and betters their behavior. In addition to these it brings them a better understanding of life.

2

Basic Principles

2

Basic
Principles

Like engineering, Scientology has certain basic principles. These are necessary to a full understanding of the subject. It is not enough to know how to process people in Scientology. To be effective one must also know the basic principles. Scientology is very exact. The humanities of the past were full of opinions. Scientology is full of facts that work.

To study Scientology one should scan quickly through the basics and find something with which one can agree. Having found *one thing* with which he can agree, one should then skim through again and find another fact. One should continue to do this until he feels some friendliness to the subject. When one has achieved this, and *only* when one has achieved this, he should then study all the basic principles. There is no effort here to be authoritarian.[1] No one will try to make the subject difficult.

You may have been taught that the mind is a very difficult thing to know about. This is the first principle of Scientology: It is possible to know about the mind, the spirit and life.

---

1. **authoritarian:** favoring complete obedience to authority as opposed to individual freedom.

The Cycle of Action

The most fundamental idea in Scientology is called the *cycle of action*.

Cycle = a span of time with a beginning and an end = a section of the totality of time with a beginning and an end = in beginningless and endless time one can set out periods which do have a beginning and an end insofar as action is concerned.

Action = motion or movement = an act = a consideration that motion has occurred.

In very ancient books it is written that from chaos came birth, from birth there was growth, when growth was achieved there was then a gradual decay, the decay then ended in death. After death there was chaos.

Scientology expresses this more briefly. The cycle of action is an apparency as follows: *create*, then *survive*, then *destroy*; or creation, survival, destruction. First there is creation. Then this is followed by survival. Then this is followed by destruction.

Apparency = appears to be, as distinct from what actually *is*.

This cycle is only an *apparency*. It is what we see, what we behold,[2] what we believe. We *consider* that it is so and then we see it so.

A child is born, he grows, he reaches manhood, he grows old, he dies. In Scientology it can be seen that none of these

---

2. **behold:** observe; look at; see.

steps are necessary. One considers them so, and so they are "true." A man can grow old quickly or slowly. He grows old to the degree that he believes he is growing old. Because everyone *agrees* that this is the way things are, they go that way. The cycle is not *true*. It is only *apparent*. It is apparent because we believe we see it. It is apparent because we *agree* that it should be so.

The test of this principle is as follows: By using the cycle of action can we make anyone well or more intelligent? Thousands of tests have proven that the use of and belief in the cycle of action has made none well or intelligent. Therefore, no matter if we see it, there must be something wrong with it. The woman, growing old, wishing to appear younger, is protesting this cycle of action. She feels there is something wrong with it. There is. We have to find out what the *actual* cycle is before we can make people better.

Actual = what is really true = that which exists despite all apparencies = that which underlies the way things seem to be = the way things really are.

The actual cycle of action is as follows: create, create-create-create, create–counter-create, no creation, nothingness.

Create = make, manufacture, construct, postulate,[3] bring into beingness[4] = *create*.

---

3. **postulate:** to generate or think a concept. A concept is a thought, and to postulate infers a requirement that something *is* something or that it isn't something or that some action is going to take place. In other words, *postulate* infers conditions and actions rather than just plain thought. (Note to translators: Lacking a proper English word for "causative thinking," the word *postulate* has been used in slight difference to its English definition. If there is a word in your language which means "self-impulsion" or "creation of a thought," use that instead of *postulate*.)

4. **beingness:** condition or state of being; existence.

Create-create-create = create again continuously one moment after the next = *survival.*

Create–counter-create = to create something against a creation = to create one thing and then create something else against it = *destroy.*

No creation = an absence of any creation = no creative activity.

An actual cycle of action then consists of various activities, but each and every one of them is creative. The cycle of action contains an apparency of survival, but this is actually only a continuous creation. The apparent cycle of action contains destruction, but the actual cycle of action tells us what destruction is. Destruction is one of *two* activities. Destruction is (in terms of action) a creation of something against a creation of something else. For example, a wall is seen standing. To be apparent it is necessary that the wall be constantly created. The act of "destruction" is to exert against the wall another creativeness, that is, the action or activity of knocking the wall down. Both the wall standing there and the action of knocking it down are "creative" actions. Because we may object to a wall being knocked down, we vilify[5] the creativeness involved in knocking it down with the word *destructive. Actuality* tells us that there is no such thing as destruction. There is only creation against a creation. There is another "type of destruction" and this is *no more creation.* By no longer being a party[6] to the wall's creation, the wall, in theory, can cease to exist for one. This is true in actual practice in Scientology.

---

5. **vilify:** to use abusive or slanderous language about.

6. **party:** a person or group that participates in some action, affair, plan, etc.; participant.

Reality is the way things appear. Reality is apparency. To do anything about reality, one must search into and discover what underlies the *apparency.* Of what does reality consist? We *see* an apparency which has the cycle of action of create-survive-destroy. More basically this cycle of action contains nothing but *creation.*

If one stops making something completely and ceases to be a party to its manufacture, it no longer exists for one. If one ceases to create, there is nothingness. When one creates something or beholds something which is created, that thing is still being created. Even if one is creating something with his left hand and has forgotten about it with his right hand, the thing still exists. In other words, one can create something without knowing it is still being created. Then one seeks to *destroy* it by a counter-creation (a creation against it). The result is a chaos created by two opposing creations.

Let us be practical. A science is not a science unless it is practical. A theory is no good unless it works. All the fancy and beautiful theory in the world is useless unless it has a use or a workability. Is this cycle of action theory useful? It is. So long as we believe that we have to destroy with force in order to destroy at all, as long as we think in terms of destruction, we have chaos.

There is creating and knowing one is creating. There is creating and not knowing one is creating. When one drives a car or a cart he does many things which he is not aware of, and these we call automatic actions. One is doing something and is not aware that he is doing it. One starts to create something, then places this thought still active beyond his own reach and the creation continues to occur.

Knowingly creating something is always the first condition.

One can then purposefully continue the creation unknowingly. Everything one is doing knowingly or unknowingly, one is doing here and now, in the present instant, in present time. One knowingly started any creation in some *past* moment. But the creation is being done in the present moment.

To stop any creation it can be established that one once knew one was creating it—finding that thought and making it known again—or one can simply create newly and consciously what one is already creating unconsciously. In either case the creation stops. The *wrong way* is to start a new creation to counter against the old creation; when one does this he gets confusion and chaos.

For example, a man has a bad leg. He is trying to "get well." He seeks, then, to create a good leg. He goes to doctors and wants to be healed. The treatment is difficult and usually somewhat unsuccessful in the case of a very severely crippled leg. *Something* is creating a bad leg. Against this he is creating a good leg. The result is confusion and a bad leg. *But* a third creativeness is present. First something was creating, we hope, a good leg. Then a counter-creation (such as an accident to his leg) counter-created a bad leg. Now he is trying to counter-create again a good leg. The result is to wipe out the original good leg since that is the creation he is taking over and exposing with his efforts to get well. He wants a good leg. The trouble with him is the counter-creation of a bad leg. The test is factual. Have him create (by a certain Scientology process) bad legs until the counter-creation of bad legs is wiped out and the original creation of a good leg will reappear. This only fails when there is no original creation of a good leg, when the original creation of a good leg is gone.

For example, a man has a job. He works at it. That is to say he create-create-creates a job throughout the days, weeks and years. As long as he makes a job, the job exists. One day he depends upon (takes for granted) this job. He no longer creates it. It ceases to exist. He has no job. The *apparency* is that he loafed and was discharged. The *actuality* is that he no longer created a job and so didn't have one.

For example, a man depends upon a woman to keep his house for him. One day he no longer has a woman. He can't keep house *even though before he married the woman he could keep house.*

For example, a man is sane. He gets the idea that it would be better to be insane. He starts to go insane (having created it) and then does numberless things in order to stay sane. Here he was already creating the state of sanity. He counter-created insanity. He then counter-created sanity against insanity.

Creation, in this work, may be thought to exclude God. We are here considering only those things which man or man as a spirit can make or manufacture or think. The subject of *who* or *what* is doing the creation does not invalidate the cycle. This is a work on the subject of the mind, not a work on the subject of the Supreme Being.

Lying is the lowest order of creativity.

There are many tests for these principles in Scientology. Such tests come under the heading of processing.

3

The
Conditions
of Existence

3

The Conditions of Existence

There are three conditions of existence.

These three conditions comprise life.

They are *be*, *do* and *have*.

The condition of being is defined as the assumption[1] of a category of identity. It could be said to be the role in a game and an example of beingness could be one's own name. Another example would be one's profession. Another example would be one's physical characteristics. Each or all of these things could be called one's *beingness*. Beingness is assumed by oneself or given to one's self, or is attained. For example, in the playing of a game each player has his own beingness.

The second condition of existence is *doing*. By *doing* we mean action, function, accomplishment, the attainment of goals, the fulfilling of purpose or any change of position in space.

The third condition is *havingness*. By *havingness* we mean owning, possessing, being capable of commanding, positioning,

---

1. **assumption:** the act of taking possession of something.

taking charge of objects, energies or spaces.

The essential definition of *having* is to be able to touch or permeate or to direct the disposition of.

The game of life demands that one assume a beingness in order to accomplish a doingness in the direction of havingness.

These three conditions are given in an order of seniority where life is concerned. The ability to be is more important than the ability to do. The ability to do is more important than the ability to have. In most people all three conditions are sufficiently confused that they are best understood in reverse order. When one has clarified the idea of possession or havingness, one can then proceed to clarify doingness for general activity, and when this is done one understands beingness or identity.

It is an essential to a successful existence that each of these three conditions be clarified and understood. The ability to assume or to grant beingness is probably the highest of human virtues. It is even more important to be able to permit other people to have beingness than to be able oneself to assume it.

Beingness = Identity

If you ask an auditor how these work in processing, he will tell you that there is a specialized form of each of these conditions. The auditing form of beingness is identity. To achieve a betterment of beingness and the granting of beingness, the auditor remedies with processing the scarcity of identities of the preclear.[2] The preclear is often found in valences:[3] his father's or

---

2. **preclear:** a person who, through Scientology processing, is finding out more about himself and life.

3. **valences:** personalities. Theoretically a person could have his own valence. But,
(continued on next page)

---

mother's or marital partner's or any or all of thousands of possible people. He is unable to achieve or obtain (he thinks) enough identity or an identity of his own. He decries[4] or criticizes the identities of others (fails to grant beingness to them).

He himself cannot obtain enough identity to feel he has an identity. Identity is so scarce that it's too valuable. Nobody must have one. To be with such a person is therefore an uncomfortable experience since he does not credit our identity—does not grant us beingness.

The "cure" for this is elementary. Let us say he is obviously in Father's valence (identity). He got into Father's valence when he found he could get no attention from Mother. Observing that Father got some of her attention, he took Father's identity. However, let us say he didn't like Father. The auditor finds him hating "himself." "Himself" is really Father.

A clever auditor (see Chapter Eleven) would see that while he was in Father's valence, it was really Mother's attention that was sought.

The auditor does not inform his preclear of such a finding. He asks the preclear to lie about (lowest form of creativity) identities which would attract Mother's attention. Then, when the preclear can do this, the auditor would have him invent identities which would attract Mother's attention.

---

more familiarly, the term is used to denote the borrowing of the personality of another. The word *valence* means, in Latin, "strength" *(valentia)*. We use it in Dianetics and Scientology as meaning personality, but it has not escaped the value of strength. A person takes at will the valences of a commanding nature or valences of a very obedient nature in order to answer up to various situations.

4. **decries:** speaks out against strongly and openly; denounces.

Suddenly the preclear would be no longer in Father's valence. However, he would have been not only in Father's but also in Mother's valence so the same process would have to be done on Father. "Lie about," the auditor would say, "identities which would attract Father's attention," then "invent one," until the preclear had many and would no longer be in Mother's valence.

Solving father and mother valences is fundamental, since most people are somewhat "in them" or revolted from them. But people can be "stuck" in all sorts of identities, even bedposts when humans are too valuable to be used.

The rule is that the more a person is "stuck" in a valence or identity, the fewer he conceives to exist. And the harder he thinks it is to get attention. Thus he can become exhibitionistic (displaying himself too thoroughly, being too much *there* at all times) or he can become dispersed (hiding himself, being vague, *not there* most of the time).

People err, in identity, in being too apparent or too little apparent. The remedy of either is the remedy of their scarcity of identity.

Identity and Attention

One "needs" an identity to play the game, as covered later, but mainly to "get attention."

A being looks at things. To balance the flow[5] of his attention, he feels he must also be looked at. Thus he becomes attention-hungry.

Unlike yellow and brown people, the white does not usually

---

5. **flow:** impulse or direction of thought, energy or action.

believe he can get attention from matter or objects. The yellow and brown believe for the most part (and it is all a matter of consideration) that rocks, trees, walls, etc., can give them attention. The white man seldom believes this and so is likely to become anxious about people.

Thus the white saves people, prevents famine, flood, disease and revolution for *people* as the *only* purveyors[6] of attention are scarce. The white goes further. He often believes he can get attention only from whites and that yellow and brown peoples' attention is worthless. Thus the yellow and brown races are not very progressive, but, by and large, saner. And the white race is progressive but more frantic. The yellow and brown races do not understand white concern for "bad conditions" since what are a few million dead men? There are *plenty* of identities and there is plenty of attention, they think. The white can't understand them. Nor can they understand the white.

Attention and identity form a group of two. Attention makes space. Identity closes space.

Attention is a method of knowing. Inattention is a method of not-knowing.

Identity is a method of making known. Lack of identity is a method of making unknown.

Valences

The whole study of valences is a fascinating one. A valence is defined as "a false identity assumed unwittingly." An identity is modified by valences. People who can be nobody may try to be everybody. People who are seeking a way out of scarcity of

---

6. **purveyors:** providers or suppliers.

identity may become fixed in false valences. Nations can become fixed in valences of countries they have conquered in war, etc., etc.

A rule is that a person assumes the identity of that which gets attention. Another rule is that the person assumes the identity of that which makes him fail. (For he gave it *his* attention, didn't he?)

There *is* a basic personality,[7] a person's *own* identity. He colors or drowns this with valences as he loses or wins in life. He *can* be dug up.

Do = Effect

Doing can be defined as the action of creating an effect. An effect in creation is action.

An auditor, processing a preclear, would always use "effect processes" to increase doingness.

"What effect could you create on Father?" would be a typical auditor question.

If a preclear is fixated by books, a machine, a tool, a person, the auditor asks him to lie about, then invent effects he could create upon it. At first the preclear may be able to think of none. Then as the process is continued he may become wildly imaginative or even cruel. Further running will bring the preclear into a more comfortable frame of mind.

---

7. **basic personality:** the individual himself. The basic individual is not a buried unknown or a different person, but an intensity of all that is best and most able in the person.

Criminals or maniacs are people who are frantically attempting to create an effect long after they know they cannot. They cannot then create decent effects, only violent effects. Neither can they work (do).

Despair of creating an effect brings about aberration[8] and irrational conduct. It also brings about laziness and carelessness.

Command of attention is necessary to creating an effect. Therefore, when one conceives he cannot easily get attention, he seeks to create stronger effects. He creates effects to get attention. He gets attention to create effects.

As in Axiom[9] 10 (given later), the creation of an effect is the highest purpose in this universe. Thus when one cannot create effects, he has no purpose. And thus it works out in life. It may be all right to be a stern and unrelenting[10] superior or parent, but such create laziness and criminals. If one cannot have an effect created upon one (and one is known to another), very definitely harmful results will ensue.

As one believes he creates the *least* effect upon unconscious or dead people, these, as in hospitals or China, become the subject of much aberrated activity. "What effect could you create

---

8. **aberration:** a departure from rational thought or behavior. From the Latin, *aberrare*, to wander from; Latin, *ab*, away, *errare*, to wander. It means basically to err, to make mistakes, or more specifically, to have fixed ideas which are not true. The word is also used in its scientific sense. It means departure from a straight line. If a line should go from A to B, and it is "aberrated," it would go from A to some other point, to some other point, to some other point, to some other point, to some other point and finally arrive at B. Taken in its scientific sense, it would also mean the lack of straightness or to see crookedly as, for example, a man sees a horse but thinks he sees an elephant. Aberrated conduct would be wrong conduct, or conduct not supported by reason. Aberration is opposed to sanity, which would be its opposite.

9. **axiom:** statement of natural law on the order of those of the physical sciences.

10. **unrelenting:** not easing or slackening in severity.

on an unconscious person (or a dead person)?" asked over and over by an auditor obtains some astonishing results.

An artist stops his work when he believes he can no longer create an effect.

A person actually dies for lack of effect.

But security often depends on being able to create *no* effect.

The whole subject of survival is bound up in no-effect. Obviously those things on which no-effect can be made, survive.

If one is anxious about survival (a foolish thing, for he can't do anything else) he becomes anxious to have about him things which resist all effects. But as his only anxiety is about the survival of a *valence* or identity, remedy of the scarcity of these can resolve the matter.

Another cycle of action containing also the classes of effects is *start, change* and *stop*. This is the definition of control.

Havingness

As there must be a playing field (see Chapter Twelve) for a game to be held, so there must be havingness. One must be able to possess.

There are millions of methods of possession in life. The obvious one becomes overlooked. If one can see a thing he can have it—if he thinks he can.

The degree to which one can live is the degree to which one can own. To own is not to label or cart away. To own is to be able to see or touch or occupy.

One loses to the degree he is forbidden to have.

But to play a game one must be able to believe he can't have.

Effect and Have

Effect and have form a pair like attention and identity.

An effect should be on or against something. Thus having-ness. If one's attention never meets anything he doesn't always like it. Thus he wants objects.

Effect makes distance. Have shortens distance.

Problems

Man or any life form in this universe seems to love problems. A problem is more important than freedom. Problems keep up interest.

When a man *has* a problem very thoroughly and can't solve it, he really has too few problems. He needs more.

The insanity among the idle is a matter of problem scarcity.

A problem is defined as two or more purposes in opposition. Or intention versus intention.

Out of the conditions of existence above can come many complex problems.

If a man had *all* the attention in the world he would be unhappy. If he had all the identities possible, he would still be unhappy. If he could blow up Earth or create any other huge effect he wanted (without limit), he would be miserable (or as insane). If he could own *everything* everywhere he would be dulled to apathy. Or so it seems. For these conditions of existence are all subordinate[11] to the need of problems, by current Scientology reasoning and results.

Thus to have a person lie about problems or invent problems of the same size as the ones he has, or the valence he is in or to invent data of the same or different size as the one he is fixed upon is to make a well man.

Probably the problem is the antidote to unconsciousness. It is certainly the antidote for boredom.

But in making up the problems of life he consults the conditions of existence: be, do, have and their necessary partner in every case, attention.

---

11. **subordinate:** of less importance; secondary.

4

The Eight Dynamics

4

The
Eight
Dynamics

$\mathbf{A}$s one looks out across the confusion which is life or existence to most people, one can discover eight main divisions, to each of which apply the conditions of existence. Each division contains a cycle of action.

There could be said to be eight urges (drives, impulses) in life. These we call *dynamics*. These are motives or motivations. We call them *the eight dynamics*.

There is no thought or statement here that any one of these eight dynamics is more important than the others. While they are categories of the broad game of life, they are not necessarily equal to each other. It will be found among individuals that each person stresses one of the dynamics more than the others, or may stress a combination of dynamics as more important than other combinations.

The purpose in setting forth this division is to increase an understanding of life by placing it in compartments. Having subdivided existence in this fashion, each compartment can be inspected as itself and by itself in its relationship to the other compartments of life. In working a puzzle it is necessary to first take pieces of similar color or character and place them in groups. In studying a subject it is necessary to proceed in an orderly fashion. To promote this orderliness it is necessary to assume for our purposes these eight arbitrary compartments of life.

The *first dynamic* is the urge toward existence as one's self. Here we have individuality expressed fully. This can be called the *self dynamic*.

The *second dynamic* is the urge toward existence as a sexual activity. This dynamic actually has two divisions. Second dynamic (a) is the sexual act itself and the second dynamic (b) is the family unit, including the rearing of children. This can be called the *sex dynamic*.

The *third dynamic* is the urge toward existence in groups of individuals. Any group or part of an entire class could be considered to be a part of the third dynamic. The school, the society, the town, the nation, are each part of the third dynamic, and each one is a third dynamic. This can be called the *group dynamic*.

The *fourth dynamic* is the urge toward existence as mankind. Whereas the white race would be considered a third dynamic, all the races would be considered the fourth dynamic. This can be called the *mankind dynamic*.

The *fifth dynamic* is the urge toward existence of the animal kingdom. This includes all living things whether vegetable or animal. The fish in the sea, the beasts of the field or of the forest, grass, trees, flowers or anything directly and intimately motivated by life. This can be called the *animal dynamic*.

The *sixth dynamic* is the urge toward existence as the physical universe. The physical universe is composed of matter, energy, space and time. In Scientology we take the first letter of each of these words and coin a word, MEST. This can be called the *universe dynamic*.

The *seventh dynamic* is the urge toward existence as or of spirits. Anything spiritual, with or without identity, would come under the heading of the seventh dynamic. This can be called the *spiritual dynamic*.

The *eighth dynamic* is the urge toward existence as infinity. This is also identified as the Supreme Being. It is carefully observed here that the *science* of Scientology does not intrude into the dynamic of the Supreme Being. This is called the eighth dynamic because the symbol of infinity stood upright makes the numeral *8*. This can be called the *infinity* or *God dynamic*.

Scientologists usually call these by number.

The earlier science, Dianetics, included dynamics one to four. Scientology embraces dynamics one through seven as known territory, scientifically demonstrated and classified.

The difficulty of stating the exact definitions of the dynamics is entirely verbal. Originally the dynamics read "the urge toward survival as ———." As the science developed it became apparent that survival was only an apparency and only one facet of existence. Both the cycle of action and the three conditions of existence belong in each dynamic.

A further manifestation of these dynamics is that they could best be represented as a series of concentric[1] circles wherein the first dynamic would be the center and each new dynamic would

---

1. **concentric:** having a center in common.

be successively a circle outside it. The idea of space adjoining[2] enters into these dynamics.

The basic characteristic of the individual includes his ability to so expand into the other dynamics, but when the seventh dynamic is reached in its entirety one will only then discover the true eighth dynamic.

As an example of use of these dynamics, one discovers that a baby at birth is not perceptive beyond the first dynamic, but as the child grows and its interests extend it can be seen to embrace other dynamics. As a further example of use, a person who is incapable of operating on the third dynamic is incapable at once of being a part of a team and so might be said to be incapable of a social existence.

As a further comment upon the eight dynamics, no one of these dynamics from one to seven is more important than any other one of them in terms of orienting the individual. While the dynamics are not of equal importance, one to the next, the ability of an individual to assume the beingness, doingness and having-ness of each dynamic is an index of his ability to live.

The eight dynamics are used in Scientology communication and should be perfectly learned as part of the language of Scientology. The abilities and shortcomings of individuals can be understood by viewing their participation in the various dynamics.

---

2. **adjoining:** being in contact at some point or line; located next to another; bordering.

5

The
ARC
Triangle

5

The ARC Triangle

There is a triangle of considerable importance in Scientology, and understanding of it gives a much greater understanding of life and an ability to use it.

The ARC triangle is the keystone[1] of living associations. This triangle is the common denominator[2] to all of life's activities. The first corner of the triangle is called affinity. The basic definition of *affinity* is the consideration of distance, whether good or bad. The most basic function of complete affinity would be the ability to occupy the same space as something else.

The word *affinity* is here used to mean love, liking or any other emotional attitude. Affinity is conceived in Scientology to be something of many facets. Affinity is a variable quality. *Affinity* is here used as a word with the context "degree of liking." Under affinity we have the various emotional tones ranged from the highest to the lowest, and these are, in part, serenity (the highest level), enthusiasm (as we proceed downward toward the baser affinities), conservatism, boredom, antagonism, anger, covert hostility, fear, grief, apathy. This, in

---

1. **keystone:** something on which associated things depend.
2. **common denominator:** a characteristic, element, etc., held in common.

Scientology, is called the tone scale. Below apathy, affinity proceeds into solidities such as matter. Affinity is conceived to be comprised first of thought, then of emotion which contains energy particles, and then as a solid.

The second corner of the triangle is reality. *Reality* could be defined as "that which appears to be." Reality is fundamentally agreement. What we agree to be real is real.

The third corner of the triangle is communication. In human relationships this is more important than the other two corners of the triangle in understanding the composition of human relations in this universe. Communication is the solvent[3] for all things. It dissolves all things.

The interrelationship of the triangle becomes apparent at once when one asks, "Have you ever tried to talk to an angry man?" Without a high degree of liking and without some basis of agreement there is no communication. Without communication and some basis of emotional response there can be no reality. Without some basis for agreement and communication there can be no affinity. Thus we call these three things a triangle. Unless we have two corners of a triangle, there cannot be a third corner. Desiring any corner of the triangle, one must include the other two.

The triangle is conceived to be very spacious at the level of serenity and completely condensed at the level of matter. Thus to represent a scale for use one would draw a large triangle with a high part of the scale and succeedingly smaller triangles down to a dot at the bottom of the scale.

Affinity, reality and communication are the basis of the

---

3. **solvent:** a dissolving or disintegrating influence.

Scientology Tone Scale, which gives a prediction of human behavior as contained in *Science of Survival*.

As has already been noted, the triangle is not an equilateral[4] triangle. Affinity and reality are very much less important than communication. It might be said that the triangle begins with communication, which brings into existence affinity and reality.

The most primitive Scientology definition of communication is "cause-distance-effect."[5] The fundamental manual of communication is the book *Dianetics 55!*

ARC *are* understanding.

If you would continue a strong and able communication with someone, there must be some basis for agreement. There must be some liking for the person and then communication can exist. We can see, then, that simple talking and writing randomly without knowledge of this would not necessarily be communication. Communication is essentially something which is sent and which is received. The intention to send and the intention to receive must both be present in some degree before an actual communication can take place. Therefore one could have conditions which appeared to be communications which were not.

Original with Scientology, as are all these concepts, the ARC triangle understood is an extremely useful tool or weapon in

---

4. **equilateral:** having all sides equal [an *equilateral* triangle].

5. **cause-distance-effect:** the interchange of ideas across space. The fullest definition of communication is the consideration and action of impelling an impulse or particle from source-point across a distance to receipt-point, with the intention of bringing into being at the receipt-point a duplication and understanding of that which emanated from the source-point. The formula of Communication is Cause, Distance, Effect, with Intention, Attention and Duplication with Understanding.

human relationships. For instance, among the ARC triangle laws, a communication to be received must approximate the affinity level of the person to whom it is directed.

As people descend the tone scale they become more and more difficult to communicate with and things with which they will agree become more and more solid. Thus we have friendly discourse[6] high on the scale and war at the bottom. Where the affinity level is hate, the agreement is solid matter, and the communication . . . bullets.

6. **discourse:** communication of ideas, information, etc., especially by talking; conversation.

6

The Reason Why

6

The
Reason Why

Life can best be understood by likening it to a game. Since we are exterior to a great number of games we can regard them with a detached eye. If we were exterior to life instead of being involved and immersed in the living of it, it would look to us much like games look to us from our present vantage point.[1]

Despite the amount of suffering, pain, misery, sorrow and travail[2] which can exist in life, the reason for existence is the same reason as one has to play a game—interest, contest, activity and possession. The truth of this assertion is established by an observation of the elements of games and then applying these elements to life itself. When we do this we find nothing left wanting in the panorama[3] of life.

By *game* we mean contest of person against person, or team against team. When we say games we mean such games as baseball, polo, chess or any other such pastime. It may at one time have struck you as peculiar that men would risk bodily injury in the field of play just for the sake of "amusement." So it

---

1. **vantage point:** position which allows a clear and broad view, understanding.
2. **travail:** intense pain; agony.
3. **panorama:** a continuous series of scenes or events; constantly changing scene.

might strike you as peculiar that people would go on living or would enter into the "game of life" at the risk of all the sorrow, travail and pain just to have something to do. Evidently there is no greater curse than total idleness. Of course, there is that condition where a person continues to play a game in which he is no longer interested.

If you will but look about the room and check off items in which you are not interested, you will discover something remarkable. In a short time you will find that there is nothing in the room in which you are not interested. You are interested in everything. However, disinterest itself is one of the mechanisms of play. In order to hide something it is only necessary to make everyone disinterested in the place where the item is hidden. Disinterest is not an immediate result of interest which has worn out. Disinterest is a commodity[4] in itself. It is palpable,[5] it exists.

By studying the elements of games we find ourselves in possession of the elements of life.

Life is a game. A game consists of *freedom, barriers* and *purposes.* This is a scientific fact, not merely an observation.

Freedom exists among barriers. A totality of barriers and a totality of freedom alike are no-game conditions. Each is similarly cruel. Each is similarly purposeless.

Great revolutionary movements fail. They promise unlimited freedom. That is the road to failure. Only stupid visionaries chant of endless freedom. Only the afraid and ignorant speak of and insist upon unlimited barriers.

---

4. **commodity:** a thing of use.

5. **palpable:** clear to the mind; obvious; evident; plain.

When the relation between freedom and barriers becomes too unbalanced, an unhappiness results.

Freedom from is all right only so long as there is a place to be free *to*. An endless desire for *freedom from* is a perfect trap, a fear of all things.

Barriers are composed of inhibiting ideas, space, energy, masses and time. Freedom in its entirety would be a total absence of these things—but it would also be a freedom without thought or action, an unhappy condition of total nothingness.

Fixed on too many barriers, man yearns[6] to be free. But launched into total freedom he is purposeless and miserable.

There is *freedom among* barriers. If the barriers are known and the freedoms are known there can be life, living, happiness, a game.

The restrictions of a government, or a job, give an employee his freedom. Without known restrictions, an employee is a slave, doomed to the fears of uncertainty in all his actions.

Executives in business and government can fail in three ways and thus bring about a chaos in their department. They can:

1. seem to give endless freedom;

2. seem to give endless barriers;

3. make neither freedom nor barriers certain.

---

6. **yearns:** deeply longs or desires.

Executive competence, therefore, consists of imposing and enforcing an adequate balance between their people's freedom and the unit's barriers and in being precise and consistent about those freedoms and barriers. Such an executive adding only in himself initiative and purpose can have a department with initiative and purpose.

An employee, buying and/or insisting upon freedom only, will become a slave. Knowing the above facts he must insist upon a workable balance between freedom and barriers.

An examination of the dynamics above will demonstrate the possibility of a combination of teams. Two group dynamics can engage one another as teams. The self dynamic can ally itself with the animal dynamic against, let us say, the universe dynamic and so have a game. In other words, the dynamics are an outline of possible teams and interplays. As everyone is engaged in several games, an examination of the dynamics will plot and clarify for him the various teams he is playing on and those he is playing against. If an individual can discover that he is only playing on the self dynamic and that he belongs to no other team it is certain that this individual will lose, for he has before him seven remaining dynamics. And the self dynamic is seldom capable of besting by itself all the remaining dynamics. In Scientology we call this condition the "only one." Here is self-determinism[7] in the guise[8] of selfish determinism and here is an individual who will most certainly be overwhelmed. To enjoy life one must be willing to be some part of life.

There is the principle in Scientology called pan-determinism. This could be loosely defined as determining the activities

---

7. **self-determinism:** a condition of determining the actions of self. It is a first (self) dynamic action and leaves the remaining seven undetermined or, in actuality, in opposition to the self.

8. **guise:** general external appearance.

of two or more sides in a game simultaneously. For instance, a person playing chess is being self-determined and is playing chess against an opponent. A person who is pan-determined on the subject of chess could play both sides of the board.

A being is pan-determined about any game to which he is senior. He is self-determined only in a game to which he is junior. For instance, a general of an army is pan-determined concerning an argument between two privates or even two companies of his command. He is pan-determined in this case; but when he confronts another army, led by another general, he becomes self-determined. The game in this wise could be said to be larger than himself. The game becomes even larger than this when the general seeks to play the parts of all the political heads which should be above him. This is the main reason why dictatorship doesn't work. It is all but impossible for one man to be pan-determined about the entire system of games which comprise a nation. He starts taking sides and then to that degree becomes much less than the government which he is seeking to run.

It has been stylish in past ages to insist only upon freedom. The French Revolution[9] furnishes an excellent example for this. In the late part of the eighteenth century, the nobles of France became so self-determined against the remainder of the country and were so incapable of taking the parts of the populace that the nobles were destroyed. Immediately the populace itself sought to take over the government, and, being restrained and being intensely antipathetic to any and all restraints, their war cry became "Freedom!" They had no further restrictions or barriers. The rules of government were thrown aside. Theft and

---

9. **French Revolution:** the revolution that began in France in 1789 with the overthrow of the French royal family and ended in 1799, with Napoleon's overthrow of the governing body established in 1795.

brigandage[10] took the place of economics. The populace, there-fore, found itself in a deeper trap and discovered itself to be involved with a dictatorship which was far more restrictive than anything it had experienced before the revolution.

Although man continually uses "Freedom!" for his war cry, he only succeeds in establishing further entrapment for himself. The reason for this is a very simple one. A game consists of freedom *and* barriers *and* purposes. When man drops the idea of restrictions or barriers he loses at once control over barriers. He becomes self-determined about barriers and not pan-determined, thus he cannot control the barriers. The barriers left uncontrolled trap him then and there.

The dwindling spiral[11] of the apparency, create-survive-destroy, comes about directly when man shuns barriers. If he considers all restrictions and barriers his enemies, he is of course refusing to control them in any way and thus he starts his own dwindling spiral. A race which is educated to think in terms of freedom only is very easily entrapped. No one in the nation will take responsibility for restrictions, therefore restrictions apparently become less and less. Actually they become more and more. As these restrictions lessen, so lessens the freedom of the individual. One cannot be free from a wall unless there is a wall. Lacking any restrictions life becomes purposeless, random, chaotic.

A good manager must be capable of taking responsibility for restrictions, in that freedom, to exist, must have barriers. A

---

10. **brigandage:** plundering by brigands [bandits].

11. **dwindling spiral:** a phenomenon of the ARC triangle whereby when one breaks some affinity, a little bit of the reality goes down, and then communication goes down, which makes it impossible to get affinity as high as before; so a little bit more gets knocked off affinity, and then reality goes down, and then communication. This is the dwindling spiral in progress, until it hits the bottom—death—which is no affinity, no communication and no reality.

failure to take initiative on the subject of restrictions or barriers causes them to arise all by themselves and exist without consent or direction.

There are various states of mind which bring about happiness. That state of mind which insists only upon freedom can bring about nothing but unhappiness. It would be better to develop a thought pattern which looked for new ways to be entrapped, and things to be trapped in, than to suffer the eventual total entrapment of dwelling upon freedom only. A man who is willing to accept restrictions and barriers, and is not afraid of them, is free. A man who does nothing but fight restrictions and barriers will usually be trapped. The way to have endless war is "abandon" all war.

As it can be seen in any game, purposes become counterposed. There is a matter of purpose–counter-purpose in almost any game played in a field with two teams. One team has the idea of reaching the goal of the other and the other has the idea of reaching the goal of the first. Their purposes are at war, and this warring of purposes makes a game.

The war of purposes gives us what we call problems. A problem has the anatomy of purposes. A problem consists of two or more purposes opposed. It does not matter what problem you face or have faced, the basic anatomy of that problem is purpose–counter-purpose.

In actual testing in Scientology it has been discovered that a person begins to suffer from problems when he does not have enough of them. There is the old saw[12] that if you want a thing done, give it to a busy man to do. Similarly if you want a happy

---

12. **old saw:** an old saying, often repeated; maxim; proverb.

associate, make sure that he is a man who can have lots of problems.

Self-determinism is a condition of determining the actions of self. It is a first (self) dynamic action and leaves the remaining seven undetermined or, in actuality, in opposition to the self. Thus if one wants to take on the rest of life in a free-for-all fight, one could be entirely insistent upon total self-determinism. As the remainder of the dynamics must have a say in one's self to function, they fight at once any attempt at total self-determinism.

Pan-determinism means determining the action of self and others. It means wider determinism than self. In an aberrated fashion we see this in an effort to control all others to aggrandize[13] self. Pan-determinism is *across* determinism or determinism of two sides. If one controls both sides of a chess game one is "above" the game.

One is self-determined, then, in any situation in which he is fighting. He is pan-determined in any situation which he is controlling.

To become pan-determined, rather than only self-determined, it is necessary to view both sides.

A problem is an intention–counter-intention. It is then something that has two opposing sides. By creating problems one tends to view both sides in opposition and so becomes pan-determined.

Thus a problem only *appears* to be necessary to man. The problem is the closest reality man has to pan-determinism. In

---

13. **aggrandize:** to make greater, more powerful, richer, etc.

processing, the invention of problems then shows a wider view and so exteriorizes one from difficulty.

From this we get the oddity of a high incidence of neurosis[14] in the families of the rich. These people have very little to do and have very few problems. The basic problems of food, clothing and shelter are already solved for them. We would suppose, then, if it were true that an individual's happiness depended only upon his freedom, these people would be happy. However, they are not happy. What brings about their unhappiness? It is the lack of problems.

Although successful processing in Scientology would depend upon taking all three elements of games into consideration—and indeed that is the secret of bettering people: taking freedom, barriers and purposes into consideration and balancing them—it is true that you could make a man well simply by sitting down with him and asking him to invent problems one after the other. The invention of synthetic problems would be found to free his mind and make him more able. Of course, there is another factor involved in this in that it is he who is inventing the problems and therefore he is becoming pan-determined about problems rather than being in one place with all problems opposed to him.

An unhappy man is one who is considering continually how to become free. One sees this in the clerk who is continually trying to avoid work. Although he has a great deal of leisure time he is not enjoying any part of it. He is trying to avoid contact with people, objects, energies and spaces. He eventually becomes trapped in a sort of lethargy. If this man could merely change his mind and start "worrying" about how he could get

---

14. **neurosis:** an obsession or compulsion that overmasters a person's self-determinism to such a degree that it is a social liability.

more work to do, his happiness level would increase markedly. One who is plotting continually how to get out of things will be miserable. One who is plotting how to get into things has a much better chance of becoming happy.

There is, of course, the matter of being forced to play games in which one has no interest—a war into which one is drafted is an excellent example of this. One is not interested in the purposes of the war and yet one finds himself fighting it. Thus there must be an additional element, and this element is "the power of choice."

One could say, then, that life is a game and that the ability to play a game consists of tolerance for freedom and barriers and an insight into purposes, with the power of choice over participation.

These four elements—freedom, barriers, purposes and power of choice—are the guiding elements of life. There are only two factors above these, and both of them are related to these. The first is the ability to create, with, of course, its negative, the ability to uncreate; and the second is the ability to make a postulate. This, then, is the broad picture of life, and in bringing life into focus and in making it less confusing, these elements are used in its understanding.

7

The
Parts of Man

7

The
Parts of Man

The individual man is divisible into three parts.

The first of these is the spirit, called in Scientology the *Thetan*.

The second of these parts is the *Mind*.

The third of these parts is the *Body*.

Probably the greatest discovery of Scientology and its most forceful contribution to the knowledge of mankind has been the isolation, description and handling of the human spirit, accomplished in July 1952 in Phoenix, Arizona. I established along scientific rather than religious or humanitarian lines that that thing which is the person, the personality, is separable from the body and the mind at will and without causing bodily death or mental derangement.[1]

In ages past there has been considerable controversy concerning the human spirit or soul, and various attempts to control

---

1. **derangement:** condition of having been upset in arrangement, order or operation; unsettled; disordered.

man have been effective in view of his almost complete ignorance of his own identity. Latterly[2] spiritualists isolated from the person what they called the astral body,[3] and with this they were able to work for various purposes of their own. In Scientology, the spirit itself was separated from what the spiritualists called the astral body and there should be no confusion between these two things. As you know that you are where you are at this moment, so you would know if you, a spirit, were detached from your mind and body. Man had not discovered this before because, lacking the technologies of Scientology, he had very little reality upon his detachment from his mind and body; therefore, he conceived himself to be at least in part a mind and a body. The entire cult[4] of communism is based upon the fact that one lives only one life, that there is no hereafter and that the individual has no religious significance. Man at large has been close to this state for at least the last century. The state is of a very low order, excluding as it does all self-recognition.

The Spirit

The thetan is described in Scientology as having no mass, no wavelength, no energy and no time or location in space except by consideration or postulate. The spirit, then, is not a *thing*. It is the *creator* of things.

The usual residence of the thetan is in the skull or near the body. A thetan can be in one of four conditions. The first would be entirely separate from a body or bodies, or even from this universe. The second would be near a body and knowingly

---

2. **latterly:** of late, nowadays.

3. **astral body:** somebody's delusion. Astral bodies are usually mock-ups which the mystic then tries to believe real. He sees the astral body as something else and then seeks to inhabit it in the most common practices of "astral walking."

4. **cult:** devoted attachment to, or extravagant admiration for, a person, principle, etc., especially when regarded as a fad.

controlling the body. The third would be in the body (the skull) and the fourth would be an inverted condition whereby he is compulsively[5] away from the body and cannot approach it. There are degrees of each one of these four states. The most optimum of these conditions, from the standpoint of man, is the second.

A thetan is subject to deterioration. This is at first difficult to understand since the entirety of his activity consists of considering or postulating. He uses, through his postulates, various methods of controlling a body. That he does deteriorate is manifest,[6] but that he can at any moment return to an entirety of his ability is also factual. In that he associates beingness with mass and action, he does not consider himself as having an individual identity or name unless he is connected with one or more of the games of life.

The processes of Scientology can establish this for the individual with greater or lesser rapidity, and one of the many goals of processing in Scientology is to "exteriorize"[7] the individual and place him in the second condition above, since it has been discovered that he is happier and more capable when so situated.

The Mind

The *mind* is a communication and control system between the thetan and his environment. The mind is a network of communications and pictures, energies and masses, which are

---

5. **compulsively:** in a manner as if compelled, urged, driven or forced.

6. **manifest:** readily perceived by the eye or the understanding; evident; obvious; apparent; plain.

7. **exteriorize:** to bring about the state of the thetan, the individual himself, being outside his body. When this is done, the person achieves a certainty that he is himself and not his body.

---

brought into being by the activities of the thetan versus the physical universe or other thetans. A thetan establishes various systems of control so that he can continue to operate a body and through the body operate things in the physical universe, as well as other bodies. The most obvious portion of the mind is recognizable by anyone not in serious condition. This is the "mental image picture." In Scientology we call this mental image picture a *facsimile* when it is a "photograph" of the physical universe sometime in the past. We call this mental image picture a *mock-up* when it is created by the thetan or for the thetan and does not consist of a photograph of the physical universe. We call a mental image picture a *hallucination* or, more properly, an *automaticity*[8] when it is created by another and seen by self.

Various phenomena connect themselves with this entity called the mind. Some people closing their eyes see only blackness, some people see pictures. Some people see pictures made by body reactions. Some people see only black screens.[9] Others see golden lines. Others see spaces, but the keynote of the entirety of the system called the mind is postulate and perception. Easily ten thousand new, separate mental phenomena, not hitherto seen by earlier observers, have been classified in Scientology and Dianetics.

The thetan receives, by the communication system called the mind, various impressions, including direct views of the physical universe. In addition to this he receives impressions from past

8. **automaticity:** something one is doing that he is not aware he is doing or is partially aware he is doing. Non-self-determined action which ought to be determined by the individual. The individual ought to be determining an action and he is not determining it.

9. **black screens:** parts of mental image pictures where the preclear is looking at blackness.

activities and, most important, he himself, being close to a total knowingness,[10] conceives things about the past and future which are independent of immediately present stimuli.[11] The mind is not in its entirety a stimulus-response mechanism as old Marxist psychology, as once taught in universities, would have one believe. The mind has three main divisions. The first of these could be called the *analytical mind*,[12] the second the *reactive mind*[13] and the third the *somatic mind*.[14]

The Analytical Mind

The *analytical mind* combines perceptions of the immediate environment, of the past (via pictures) and estimations of the future into conclusions which are based upon the realities of situations. The analytical mind combines the potential knowingness of the thetan with the conditions of his surroundings and brings him to independent conclusions. This mind could be said to consist of visual pictures either of the past or of the physical universe, monitored by, and presided over by, the knowingness of a thetan. The keynote of the analytical mind is awareness. One knows what one is concluding and knows what he is doing.

---

10. **knowingness:** awareness not depending upon perception. One doesn't have to look to find out. For example, you do not have to get a perception or picture of where you are living to know where you live.

11. **stimuli:** things that rouse the mind or spirit or incite to activity.

12. **analytical mind:** the conscious, aware mind which thinks, observes data, remembers it and resolves problems. It would be essentially the conscious mind as opposed to the unconscious mind.

13. **reactive mind:** the portion of the mind which works on a stimulus-response basis (given a certain stimulus it will automatically give a certain response) which is not under a person's volitional control and which exerts force and power over a person's awareness, purposes, thoughts, body and actions.

14. **somatic mind:** that mind which takes care of the automatic mechanisms of the body, the regulation of the minutiae [precise details] which keep the organism running.

The Reactive Mind

The *reactive mind* is a stimulus-response mechanism, ruggedly built, and operable in trying circumstances. The reactive mind never stops operating. Pictures, of a very low order, are taken by this mind of the environment even in some states of unconsciousness. The reactive mind acts below the level of consciousness. *It* is the literal, stimulus-response mind. Given a certain stimulus it gives a certain response. The entire subject of Dianetics concerned itself mainly with this one mind.

While it is an order of thinkingness, the ability of the reactive mind to conclude rationally is so poor that we find in the reactive mind those various aberrated impulses which are gazed upon as oddities of personality, eccentricities,[15] neuroses and psychoses.[16] It is this mind which stores up all the bad things that have happened to one and throws them back to him again in moments of emergency or danger so as to dictate his actions along lines which have been considered "safe" before. As there is little thinkingness involved in this, the courses of action dictated by the reactive mind are often not safe, but highly dangerous.

The reactive mind is entirely literal in its interpretation of words and actions. As it takes pictures and receives impressions during moments of unconsciousness, a phrase uttered when a blow is struck is likely to be literally interpreted by the reactive mind and becomes active upon the body and analytical mind at later times. The mildest stage of this would be arduous training, wherein a pattern is laid into the mind for later use under certain given stimuli.

---

15. **eccentricities:** deviations from what is ordinary or customary, as in conduct or manner; oddities; unconventionalities.

16. **psychoses:** major forms of mental affliction or disease. A psychotic is an individual who cannot handle himself or his environment well enough to survive and who must be cared for to protect others from him or to protect him from himself.

A harsh and less workable level is the hypnotic trance condition to which the mind is susceptible. Made impressionable by fixed attention, words can be immediately implanted into the reactive mind which become operable under restimulation[17] at later times.

An even lower level in the reactive mind is that one associated with blows, drugs, illness, pain and other conditions of unconsciousness. Phrases spoken over an anesthetized person can have a later effect upon that person. It is not necessarily true that each and every portion of an operation is painstakingly "photographed" by the reactive mind of the unconscious patient, but it is true that a great many of these stimuli are registered. Complete silence, in the vicinity of a person under anesthetic or a person who is unconscious or in deep pain, is mandatory if one would preserve the mental health of that person or patient afterwards.

Probably the most therapeutic action which could occur to an individual would be, under Scientology processing, the separation of the thetan from the mind so that the thetan, under no duress and with total knowingness, could view himself and his mind and act accordingly. However, there is a type of exteriorization which is the most aberrative of all traumatic[18] actions. This is the condition when an individual is brought, through injury or surgery or shock, very close to death so that he exteriorizes from body and mind. This exteriorization under duress is sudden, and, to the patient, inexplicable, and is in itself very shocking. When this has occurred to an individual, it is certain that he will suffer mentally from the experience afterwards.

---

17. **restimulation:** the reactivation of a past memory due to similar circumstances in the present approximating circumstances of the past.

18. **traumatic:** of or pertaining to a shocking or startling experience that has a lasting mental effect.

It could be said that when the reactive mind contains these sudden shocks of exteriorization under duress, attempts to exteriorize the individual later by Scientology are more difficult. However, modern processing has overcome this. The phenomenon of exteriorization under duress is accompanied at times by energy explosions in the various facsimiles of the mind, and these cross-associate in the reactive mind. Therefore, people become afraid of exteriorization, and at times people are made ill simply by discussing the phenomenon, due to the fact that they have exteriorized under duress during some operation or accident.

Exteriorization under duress is the characteristic of death itself. Therefore, exteriorization or the departure of the soul is generally associated with death in the minds of most people. It is not necessarily true that one is dead because he exteriorizes, and it is definitely not true that exteriorization not accompanied by a shock, pain or duress is at all painful. Indeed, it is quite therapeutic.

The Somatic Mind

The third portion of the mind is the *somatic mind*. This is an even heavier type of mind than the reactive mind since it contains no thinkingness and contains only actingness. The impulses placed against the body by the thetan through various mental machinery arrive at the voluntary, involuntary and glandular[19] levels. These have set methods of analysis for any given situation and so respond directly to commands given.

Unfortunately, the somatic mind is subject to each of the minds higher in scale above it and to the thetan. In other words,

19. **glandular:** of, like or functioning as a gland (any organ or specialized group of cells that separates certain elements from the blood and secretes them in a form for the body to use or throw off).

the thetan can independently affect the somatic mind. The analytical mind can affect the somatic mind. The reactive mind can affect the somatic mind. Thus we see that the neurons,[20] the glandular system, the muscles and masses of the body are subject to various impulses, each one of a lower order than the next. Thus it is not odd to discover what we call "psychosomatic"[21] illness. A condition exists here where the thetan does not have an awareness of burdening the somatic mind with various commands or derangements. Neither does the thetan have an awareness of his own participation in the analytical mind causing this action against the body.

In that the thetan is seldom aware of the reactive mind, it is possible, then, for the reactive mind, with its stimulus-response content, to impinge itself directly and without further recourse[22] or advice upon the neurons, muscles and glandular system of the body. In that the reactive mind can hold a fixed command in place, causing a derangement in the somatic mind, it is possible, then, for illness to exist, for bizarre pains to be felt, for actual physical twists and aberrations to occur, without any conscious knowledge on the part of the thetan. This we call physical illness caused by the mind. In brief, such illness is caused by perceptions received in the reactive mind during moments of pain and unconsciousness.

Whether the facsimile in the mind is received while the thetan is awake or unconscious, the resulting mass of the energy picture is energy just as you see energy in an electric light bulb or from the flames of a fire. At one time it was considered

---

20. **neurons:** the structural and functional units of the nervous system.

21. **psychosomatic:** *psycho* refers to mind and *somatic* refers to body; the term *psychosomatic* means the mind making the body ill or illnesses which have been created physically within the body by derangement of the mind.

22. **recourse:** applying or going to for help, advice or information.

that mental energy was different from physical energy. In Scientology it has been discovered that mental energy is simply a finer, higher level physical energy. The test of this is conclusive in that a thetan "mocking up" mental image pictures and thrusting them into the body can increase the body mass and, by casting them away again, can decrease the body mass. This test has actually been made and an increase of as much as thirty pounds, actually measured on scales, has been added to, and subtracted from, a body by creating "mental energy." Energy is energy. It has different wavelengths and different characteristics. The mental image pictures are capable of reacting upon the physical environment, and the physical environment is capable of reacting upon mental image pictures. Thus the mind actually consists of spaces, energies and masses of the same order as the physical universe, if lighter and different in size and wavelength. For a much more comprehensive picture of the mind one should read *The Dynamics of Life—An Introduction to Dianetics Discoveries* and *Dianetics: The Modern Science of Mental Health.* These were written before the discoveries of the upper levels of beingness were made and are a very complete picture of the mind itself, its structure and what can be done to it and with it.

The Body

The third part of man is the physical *body.* This can best be studied in such books as *Gray's Anatomy* and other anatomical[23] texts. This is the province of the medical doctor and, usually, the old-time psychiatrist or psychologist, who were involved, in the main, in body worship. The body is a purely structural study, and the actions and reactions among its various structures are complex and intensely interesting.

---

23. **anatomical:** of or connected with the structure of an organism or body.

When Scientology established biophysics,[24] it did so because of the various discoveries which had accumulated concerning mental energy in its reaction against physical energy, and the activities which took place in the body because of these interactions. Biophysics only became feasible when it was discovered in Scientology that a fixed electrical field existed surrounding a body entirely independent of, but influenceable by, the human mind. The body exists in its own space. That space is created by *anchor points*.[25] The complexity of these anchor points can cause an independent series of electronic flows which can occasion much discomfort to the individual. The balance structure of the body and even its joint action and physical characteristics can be changed by changing this electrical field which exists at a distance from, or within, the body.

The electrical field is paramount[26] and monitors the actual physical structure of the body. Thus the body is not only influenced by the three minds, it is influenced as well by its own electrical field. An expert Scientologist can discover for the average person this field, and can bring about its adjustment, although this is very far from the primary purpose of the Scientologist.

The use of electrical shocks upon a body for any purpose is therefore very dangerous and is not condoned by sensible men. Of course, the use of electrical shock was never intended to be therapeutic, but was intended only to bring about obedience by duress and, as far as it can be discovered, to make the entirety of insanity a horror. Electrical shock deranges the electronic field in

---

24. **biophysics:** the branch of physics dealing with the way the laws of physics apply to living things.

25. **anchor points:** points which demark (limit) the outermost boundaries of a space or its corners.

26. **paramount:** ranking higher than any other, as in power or importance; chief; supreme.

the vicinity of the body and is always succeeded by bad health or physical difficulties and never does otherwise than hasten the death of the person. It has been stated by people using electric shock that if they were denied euthanasia[27] they would at least use partial euthanasia in the form of electric shock, brain surgery and drugs. These treatments in some large percentage of cases, however, effected euthanasia as they were expected to do.

A knowledge of the mental and physical structure of the body would be necessary in order to treat the body, and this knowledge has not existed prior to Scientology. The medical doctor achieved many results by working purely with structure and biochemical products, and in the field of emergency surgery and obstetrics[28] and orthopedics[29] he is indispensable in the society. Medicine, however, did not even contain a definition for *mind* and is not expected to invade the field which belongs properly to Scientology.

These three parts of man—the thetan, the mind and the body—are each one different studies, but they influence each other markedly and continually. Of the three, the senior entity is the thetan, for without the thetan there would be no mind or animation in the body, while without a body or a mind there is still animation and life in the thetan. The thetan *is* the person. You are *you, in* a body.

Many speculations in the field of para-Scientology have been made. Para-Scientology includes all of the uncertainties and

27. **euthanasia:** the original definition of *euthanasia* is "mercy killing" or "easy death." However, under the practice of psychiatry it has become "the act of killing people considered a burden on society."

28. **obstetrics:** the branch of medicine concerned with the care and treatment of women during pregnancy, childbirth and the period immediately following.

29. **orthopedics:** the branch of surgery dealing with the treatment of deformities, diseases and injuries of the bones, joints, muscles, etc.

unknown territories of life which have not been completely explored and explained. However, as studies have gone forward, it has become more and more apparent that the senior activity of life is that of the thetan, and that in the absence of the spirit no further life exists. In the insect kingdom it is not established whether or not each insect is ordered by a spirit or whether one spirit orders enormous numbers of insects. It is not established how mutation[30] and evolution occur (if they do), and the general authorship of the physical universe is only speculated upon, since Scientology does not invade the eighth dynamic.

Some facts, however, are completely known. The first of these is that the individual himself is a spirit controlling a body via a mind. The second of these is that the thetan is capable of making space, energy, mass and time. The third of these is that the thetan is separable from the body without the phenomenon of death, and can handle and control a body from well outside it. The fourth of these is that the thetan does not care to remember the life which he has just lived, after he has parted from the body and the mind. The fifth of these is that a person dying always exteriorizes. The sixth of these is that the person, having exteriorized, usually returns to a planet and procures, usually, another body of the same type of race as before.

In para-Scientology there is much discussion about *between-lives areas*[31] and other phenomena which might have passed at one time or another for heaven or hell, but it is established completely that a thetan is immortal and that he himself cannot actually experience death and counterfeits it by forgetting. It is adequately manifest that a thetan lives again and that he is very

---

30. **mutation:** change or alteration, as in form or nature.

31. **between-lives areas:** the experiences of a thetan during the time between the loss of a body and the assumption of another.

anxious to put something on the *time track*[32] (something for the future) in order to have something to come back to, thus we have the anxieties of sex. There must be additional bodies for the next life.

It is obvious that what we create in our societies during this lifetime affects us during our next lifetime. This is quite different than the "belief," or the idea, that this occurs. In Scientology we have very little to do with forcing people to make conclusions. An individual can experience these things for himself and unless he can do so no one expects him to accept them.

The manifestation that our hereafter is our next life entirely alters the general concept of spiritual destiny. There is no argument whatever with the tenets[33] of faith since it is not precisely stated, uniformly, by religions that one immediately goes to a heaven or hell. It is certain that an individual experiences the effect of the civilization which he has had part in creating, in his next lifetime. In other words, the individual comes back. He has a responsibility for what goes on today since he will experience it tomorrow.

Sex has been overweighted in importance in old psychotherapy, an importance more or less disgraced at this time. Sex is only one of numerous creative impulses. An anxiety about sex, however, occurs when an individual begins to believe that there will not be a body for him to have during the next lifetime.

---

32. **time track:** the consecutive record of mental image pictures which accumulates through a person's life or lives. It is very exactly dated. The time track is the entire sequence of "now" incidents, complete with all perceptics, picked up by a person during his whole existence.

33. **tenets:** principles or beliefs held as truths.

The common denominator of all aberration is cessation[34] of creation. As sex is only one kind of creation and a rather low order of it, it will be seen that unhappiness could stem from various cessations of creation. Death itself is a cessation of creation. One stops creating the identity John Jones and the environment and things of John Jones. He stops because he believes he cannot himself continue this creation without the assistance of a body, having become dependent upon a mind and a body—the first to do his thinking for him and the second to do his acting. An individual becomes sufficiently morose[35] on the ideas of creation that he can actually bring about the condition of an inability to create.

Control

It will be seen that the three parts of man are intimately associated with *control*. The anatomy of control is start, change and stop. The loss of control takes place with the loss of pan-determinism. When one becomes too partisan,[36] braces himself too solidly against the remainder of the environment, he no longer controls the environment to the degree that he might and so is unable to start, change and stop the environment.

It is a scientific definition in Scientology that control consists of start, change and stop. These three manifestations can be graphed alongside of the apparent cycle of action: create, survive, destroy. Any person is somewhere along this curve. An individual who is bent mainly upon survival is intent, usually, upon changing things. An individual who is close to being destroyed is bent mainly upon stopping things. An individual

---

34. **cessation:** stopping, either forever or for some time.
35. **morose:** ill-tempered; gloomy, sullen, etc.
36. **partisan:** biased, prejudiced or one-sided.

who has a free heart and mind about life is bent upon creating things.

There could be three things wrong with any person, and these would be the inability to start, the inability to change, the inability to stop. Insanity, for the most part, is an inability to stop. A neurosis is a habit which, worsening, flies entirely out of control. One is stopped so often in life that he becomes an enemy of stopping and dislikes stopping so intensely that he himself will not stop things. Neurosis and psychosis of all classes are entirely inabilities to start, to change or to stop.

In the matter of the parts of man we discover that all things are initiated[37] by the thetan so far as action, activity and behavior are concerned. After such an initiation he can be blunted or warped from course and acted upon in such a way that his attention becomes too fixed along one line or another and begins to suffer from these three inabilities. However, each one of the parts of man is subject to the anatomy of control.

An individual begins first by being unable himself, without help, to start, to change and to stop. Then the mind may become prone to these disabilities and is unable to start, change or stop at will. Then the body itself can become subject to these three disabilities and is unable to start, to change and to stop. The oddity is that an environment can so work upon an individual, however, that a thetan's body becomes disabled through no choice of his own. Similarly, the reactive mind can become disabled through no choice of either the body or the thetan; but the thetan himself, beyond observing the effect of various causes and having initiated the thought to be there, can only become disabled by becoming too partisan, by becoming too little pan-determined, and so bringing himself into difficulties. These

---

37. **initiated:** brought into practice or use; introduced; started.

difficulties, however, are entirely the difficulties of consideration. As the thetan considers, so he is. In the final analysis the thetan has no problems of his own. The problems are always "other people's problems" and must exist in the mind or the body or in other people or his surroundings for him to have problems. Thus his difficulties are, in the main, difficulties of staying in the game and keeping the game going.

If a thetan can suffer from anything, it is being out-created. The manifestations of being out-created would be the destruction of his own creations and the overpowering presence of other creations. Thus a thetan can be brought to believe that he is trapped if he is out-created.

In past dissertations on the subject of the mind and philosophies of life there was a great deal of speculation and very little actual proof. Therefore, these philosophies were creations, and one philosopher was at work out-creating another philosopher. In Scientology we have this single difference. We are dealing with discoveries. The only things created about Scientology are the actual books and works in which Scientology is presented. The phenomena of Scientology are discovered and are held in common by all men and all life forms. There is no effort in Scientology to out-create each and every thetan that comes along. It is, of course, possible to conceive Scientology as a creation, and to conceive that it is overwhelming. It should be viewed otherwise, for it is intended as an assistance to life at large, to enable life to make a better civilization and a better game. There are no tenets in Scientology which cannot be demonstrated with entirely scientific procedures.

8

Causation
and Knowledge

8

Causation and Knowledge

Scientology as a science is composed of many axioms. There are some fifty-eight of these axioms in addition to the two hundred more axioms of Dianetics which preceded the Scientology axioms.

The first axiom in Scientology is

Axiom 1. Life is basically a static. (Definition: A life static has no mass, no motion, no wavelength, no location in space or in time. It has the ability to postulate and to perceive.)

Definition: In Scientology, the word postulate *means to cause a thinkingness or consideration. It is a specially applied word and is defined as causative thinkingness.*

Axiom 2. The static is capable of considerations, postulates and opinions.

Axiom 3. Space, energy, objects, form and time are the result of considerations made and/or agreed upon or not by the static, and are perceived solely because the static considers that it can perceive them.

Axiom 4. Space is a viewpoint of dimension. (Space is caused by looking out from a point. The only actuality of space is the agreed-upon consideration that one perceives through something, and this we call space.)

Axiom 5. Energy consists of postulated particles in space. (One considers that energy exists and that he can perceive energy. One also considers that energy behaves according to certain agreed-upon laws. These assumptions or considerations are the totality of energy.)

Axiom 6. Objects consist of grouped particles and solids.

Axiom 7. Time is basically a postulate that space and particles will persist. (The rate of their persistence is what we measure with clocks and the motion of heavenly bodies.)

Axiom 8. The apparency of time is the change of position of particles in space.

Axiom 9. Change is the primary manifestation of time.

Axiom 10. The highest purpose in the universe is the creation of an effect.

These first ten axioms of Scientology are the most fundamental "truths" (by which we mean commonly held considerations). Here we have thought and life and the physical universe in their relation, one to the other. Regardless of further considerations, ideas, assumptions and conditions, there lies beneath them these first ten truths.

It is as though one had entered into an honorable bargain with fellow beings to hold these things in common. Once this is done, or once such a "contract" or agreement exists, one has the fundamentals of a universe. Specialized considerations based on the above make one or another kind of universe.

The physical universe which we see around us and in which we live was created on these fundamentals without regard to Who created it. Its creation was agreed upon. In order to perceive it, one must agree that it exists.

There are three classes of universes. There is first, foremost and most evident, the physical universe of spaces, stars, suns, land, sea, air and living forms. Then there is the other fellow's universe which may or may not be agreed upon by his associates. This he holds to himself. The phenomenon of this universe is included in the field of the "mind" as described earlier. Then, listed last here, but first perceived, is one's own universe.

The phenomenon of universes is an interesting one, since one's own universe can be overwhelmed by the universes of others. These in Scientology we call valences. Valences and universes are the same thing, essentially.

For example, one while living in the physical universe can be overpowered by the universe of, let us say, Father. While one still retains his own valence or identity, one is yet acting or thinking or suffering or feeling somewhat like Father. Even though one is by oneself, there is this additional apparent beingness. Although Father is absent, his commands are still present. Thus we get such things as "duty," "obedience," "training" and even "education." Each one of these is caused by some part of another universe to a greater or lesser degree.

Regardless of how one reacts to universes, he still remains in some degree himself. It is the effort of many to struggle against universes or valences. In fact, this is a game and the essence of games. The totality of the impulse of aberrated people is the effort to separate one's own self as a thetan from the various universes with which he feels himself too intimately associated. One is only oppressed by a universe when he feels he can have nothing of that universe. One is only victimized by "Father's universe" when one is in protest against Father. One protests against the physical universe only when he feels that he can have no part of it or does not belong in it or, as in religion, is not looked upon kindly by what he conceives to be the Creator of the physical universe. There is a basic law about universes: The postulates of the creator of any universe are the postulates which "work" in that universe. Thus one may feel uncomfortable in the universe of another.

Universes, as considered in games earlier, could be considered the playing fields of life. One plays willingly or one plays unwillingly. When one begins to play unwillingly he is apt to discover himself victimized by and interiorized[1] into the universe of some game. It is against this phenomenon that a person protests. Consider the matter of a jail. On the surface of it, as Voltaire[2] discovered, a jail provides food and shelter and leisure time. This would seem to be the ambition of many people, but the jail provides as well a restriction without one's consent. The only difference between being in jail and being the king in a castle, so far as liberty is concerned, is one's own desires in the matter and one's own ability to command one's environment. As a king in a castle one would be causative. His will, statement, thinkingness, would have an effect upon others. Being in jail, one is an effect in that the thinkingness of others finds him its target. Here we have, in terms of universes, the most rudimentary example of cause and effect.

---

1. **interiorized:** having gone into something and become a part of it too fixedly.

2. **Voltaire, François:** (1694–1778) French writer and philosopher.

We must, however, assume, because it is so evident, that an individual only gets into traps and circumstances he intends to get into. Certain it is that, having gotten into such a position, he may be unwilling to remain in it, but a trap is always preceded by one's own choice of entrance. We must assume a very wide freedom of choice on the part of a thetan, since it is almost impossible to conceive how a thetan could get himself trapped even though he consented to it. By actual demonstration a thetan goes through walls, barriers, vanishes space, appears anywhere at will and does other remarkable things. It must be, then, that an individual can be trapped only when he considers that he is trapped. In view of the fact that the totality of existence is based upon his own considerations, we find that the limitations he has must have been invited to himself, otherwise they could not be eradicated by the individual under processing, since the only one who is present with the preclear is the auditor; and past associates of the preclear, while not present, do desensitize, under auditing, in the preclear's mind. Therefore it must have been the preclear who kept them there. The preclear by processing can resolve all of his difficulties without going and finding other persons or consulting other universes. Thus, the totality of entrapment, aberration, even injury, torture, insanity and other distasteful items are basically considerations a thetan is making and holding right now in present time. This must be the case since time itself is a postulate or consideration on his own part.

The greatest philosophical clamor or quarrel has been waged around the subject of "knowledge," and there is nothing preposterous[3] on the subject of knowledge that cannot be found in the philosophical texts. The superiority and ascendancy[4] of

---

3. **preposterous:** so contrary to nature, reason or common sense as to be laughable; absurd; ridiculous.

4. **ascendancy:** position in which one has control or power; supremacy.

Scientology depends upon the fact that it has transcended[5] this philosophical quarrel on the subject of knowingness, and Scientology contains in itself the basics of knowledge.

By *knowledge* we mean assured belief, that which is known, information, instruction, enlightenment, learning, practical skill. By *knowledge* we mean data, factors and whatever can be thought about or perceived.

The reason why knowledge has been misunderstood in philosophy is that it is only half the answer. There is no allness to knowledge. By definition, *knowledge* is that which is perceived or learned or taken from another source. This patently[6] then means that when one learns he is being an effect.

We see in Axiom 10 that "The highest purpose in the universe is the creation of an effect." This is in direct contradiction to knowledge, although one of course can know how to create an effect.

Opposed to knowledge we have the neglected half of existence, which is the *creation* of knowledge, the creation of data, the creation of thought, the causative consideration, self-evolved ideas as opposed to ideas otherwise evolved. The reason Scientology is such a fascinating study is that it takes apart the other fellow's ideas and permits one to create some of his own. Scientology gives us the common denominators of objects, energies, spaces, universes, livingness and thought itself.

There is *cause* and *effect*. *Cause* could be defined as emanation. It could be defined also, for purposes of communication, as source-point. If you consider a river flowing to the sea, the place

---

5. **transcended:** gone beyond the limits of; overstepped; exceeded.

6. **patently:** clearly; obviously; openly.

where it began would be the source-point or cause, and the place where it went into the sea would be the effect-point, and the sea would be the effect of the river. The man firing the gun is cause; the man receiving the bullet is effect. The one making a statement is causing a communication; the one receiving the statement is the effect of the communication. A basic definition of *communication* is cause-distance-effect.

Almost all anxieties and upsets in human relations come about through an imbalance of cause and effect.

One must be willing at once to cause new data, statements, assumptions, considerations, and to receive ideas, assumptions, considerations.

So great is the anxiety of a thetan to cause an effect that he closely approaches those things which can cause an effect upon him. Thus a thetan becomes trapped. On the face of it, so few thetans make causative data and so many receive data that it would seem, in view of the fact that a thetan can be touched only by his own consideration, that thetans are more anxious for effects than to be cause; however, this is not true in practice. In a game one seeks to cause an effect and to receive no-effect.

It is learned under close experiment that there is nothing a thetan actually disdains[7] on an effect level. He pretends not to like or enjoy certain effects and protests against them, but he knows very well that the mechanism of protest causes the effect to approach more closely as a general rule. This came about by his repeated failure in games. Insisting on no-effect for himself, he lost. Then he had to say he liked the effect.

---

7. **disdains:** thinks unworthy of notice, response, etc.; considers beneath oneself.

The prevailing anxiety, then, is to be an effect, not to be a cause. The entire subject of responsibility is a study of cause and effect in that a person who wants no responsibility is anxious to be an effect only, and a person who can assume responsibility must also be willing to be causative.

A thetan can be swung into a "state of consideration" by observing that it is commonly held by others. This keeps him in the universe and this keeps him being effect.

Study, investigation, receiving education and similar activity are all effect activities and result in the assumption of less responsibility. Thus, while it is true that a thetan cannot actually get into trouble, he can, by agreeing with the current agreed-upon thought in the universe where he finds himself, take a pattern of thinkingness which makes him less effective because he wishes to be an effect. If he feels he must gather all of his data from elsewhere, he is then the effect of knowledge, the effect of universes and postulates, and he tends to reduce his own ability to form or make knowledge.

In Scientology we can communicate in full these circumstances since we are only calling to attention the pattern which an individual already himself holds, thus we are not actually teaching him anything. We are only pointing out things he has already agreed with or himself caused.

It is only generally true that an individual is responsible for everything that happens to him. When an individual, wishing to cause many interesting effects, chooses to go into many universes or traps, he can become confused about what he is doing, where he is or what it is all about. Scientology points out that this can be seen or changed from a person's own viewpoint to bring about a change in his own condition.

As an example, a thetan has come to "believe" that the right way to get along in life is to do just as Father did. This is an invitation to being in Father's universe. Later on he changes his mind about this, but he finds himself still in Father's universe and doesn't like it. He would be more effective, more capable, if he were not now in Father's universe. Customarily, in these unenlightened times, he waits for death to separate himself from the environment in which he finds himself and puts up with it until then. It is not necessary to do this now that we have Scientology. He can at any moment, given the proper steerage,[8] vacate any trap in which he finds himself and begin again on a new series of considerations.

We cannot then talk about knowledge as a totality. It is a single datum. The thirst for knowledge would be the thirst for other thetans' postulates and would lead one to forget that he himself has been a party to the making of these postulates and that he himself had to follow a certain course in order to put himself in reach of other thetans' postulates.

Because one is the effect of knowledge, the causing of data, considerations or "facts" to come into existence separates one in distance from being an effect, if one is very anxious to be an effect. If this is his basic consideration, he will not take well to causing information to come into existence, but in order to get him out of the traps in which he finds himself, it is necessary to some degree that he do so.

Causing few barriers or traps, the individual then loses control over barriers or traps, wishing to be a no-effect. Of course, he does lose control of barriers and traps; otherwise he cannot be entrapped by them. The thing to do to free him from a trap is to find what parts of the trap he himself is willing to create, own or have or possess. This places the barriers (which can be spaces,

8. **steerage:** the act of steering.

energy movements or obstacles) under his control; and his pos-tulating that he can have or possess this or that causes him to be willing to be or occupy the trap. The moment this occurs he is no longer in the trap, or even if he is still in it to some degree he does not object to it and can leave it when he wishes.

Civilization and Savagery

The way to paralyze a nation entirely and to make it com-pletely ungovernable would be to forbid education of any kind within its borders and to inculcate[9] into every person within it the feeling that he must not receive any information from any-body about anything. To make a nation governable it is necessary to hold a kindly view of education and to honor educative persons and measures. To conquer a land it is not necessarily efficient to overwhelm it with guns. Once this is done it is necessary to apply educative measures in order to bring about some sort of agreement among the people themselves, as well as between the conqueror and the subdued. Only in this way could one have a society, a civilization or, as we say in Scientology, a smoothly running game.

In other words, two extremes could be reached, neither one of which is desirable by the individual. The first extreme could be reached by emphasis only upon self-created data or informa-tion. This would bring about not only a lack of interpersonal relations, but also an anxiety to have an effect which would, as it does in barbaric peoples, result in social cruelty unimaginable in a civilized nation. The other extreme would be to forbid in its entirety any self-created information and to condone only data or considerations generated by others than self. Here we would

---

9. **inculcate:** to impress upon the mind by frequent repetition or persistent urging.

create an individual with no responsibility, so easily handled that he would be only a puppet.

Self-created data is, then, not a bad thing, neither is education, but one without the other to hold it in some balance will bring about a no-game condition or a no-civilization. Just as individuals can be seen, by observing nations, so we see the African tribesman, with his complete contempt for truth and his emphasis on brutality and savagery for others but not himself, is a no-civilization. And we see at the other extreme China, slavishly dedicated to ancient scholars, incapable of generating within herself sufficient rulers to continue, without bloodshed, a nation.

We have noted the individual who must be the only one who can make a postulate or command, whose authority is dearer to him than the comfort or state of millions that have suffered from such men (Napoleon,[10] Hitler,[11] Kaiser Wilhelm,[12] Frederick of Prussia,[13] Genghis Khan,[14] Attila[15]). We have

---

10. **Napoleon Bonaparte:** (1769–1821) French military leader. He rose to power in France by military force, declared himself emperor and conducted campaigns of conquest across Europe until his final defeat by armies allied against him in 1815.

11. **Hitler, Adolf:** (1889–1945) dictator of Germany from 1933 to 1945. In rising to power in Germany, he fortified his position through murder of real or imagined opponents and maintained police-state control over the population. He led Germany into World War II resulting in its nearly total destruction.

12. **Kaiser Wilhelm:** William II (1859–1941), emperor of Germany from 1888 to 1918. (*Kaiser* is German for "emperor.") Through inept handling of his power and authority as emperor, he helped cause the circumstances leading to World War I and thereby the deaths of millions of men on the battlefields.

13. **Frederick of Prussia:** (1712–86) king of Prussia. Known as Frederick the Great, he conducted intermittent campaigns of conquest into neighboring countries. The wars he took his country into eventually involved all of Europe.

14. **Genghis Khan:** (1162–1227) Mongol conqueror of much of Asia and Eastern Europe. His armies were totally ruthless in their actions and were said to have killed over a million people in one city alone.

15. **Attila:** (406?–53) king of the Huns, a nomadic and warlike Asian people who invaded and controlled large parts of Eastern and Central Europe.

known, too, the scholar who has studied himself into blindness and is the world's greatest authority on government or some such thing, who yet cannot himself manage his bank account or a dog with any certainty. Here we have, in either case, a total imbalance. The world shaker is himself unwilling to be any effect of any kind (and all the men named here were arrant[16] personal cowards), and we have the opposite, a man who would not know what you were talking about if you told him to get an idea of his own.

We see another example of this in the fundamental laws of warfare. A body of troops, to be effective, must be able to attack and to defend. Its implements must be divided fifty percent for attack and fifty percent for defense. In other words, even in a crude activity such as warfare, we find that no successful outcome is possible unless the troops can devote half of their energies to attack and half of them to defense.

In the much broader view of life we discover on any dynamic that success or a game or activity or life itself depends upon being willing to be cause as well as willing to be an effect. He who would give must be willing to receive. He who would receive must be willing to give. When these tenets are violated, the most fundamental principle of human relationships is violated, and the result is a no-game condition such as aberration, insanity, antisocialness, criminality, inactivity, laziness, tiredness, mania,[17] fanaticism and all the other things against which men protest. But imbalances between cause and effect also enter randomities[18] into the game of life and cannot be neglected in

---

16. **arrant:** that is plainly such; out-and-out; notorious.

17. **mania:** excessive excitement or enthusiasm.

18. **randomities:** things one picks out and agrees not to predict. Randomity is a consideration of motion. A person can have too much or too little motion, or enough motion. What is enough motion is measured by the consideration of the individual.

their potential for creating a game.

Any information is valuable to the degree that you can use it. In other words, any information is valuable to the degree that you can make it yours. Scientology, of all the sciences, does not teach you—it only reminds you, for the information was yours in the first place. It is not only the science of life, but it is an account of what you were doing before you forgot what you were doing.

9

Know
and Not-Know

9

Know and Not-Know

It is a mechanism of thinkingness, whether one is postulating or receiving information, that one retain one's ability to know. It is equally important that one retain one's ability to not-know. Thought consists entirely of knowing and not-knowing and the shades of gray between.

You will discover that most people are trying not to remember. In other words, they are trying to not-know. Education can only become burdensome when one is unable to not-know it. It is necessary that one be able to create, to receive, to know and to not-know information, data and thoughts. Lacking any one of these skills, for they are skills, no matter how native they are to the individual, one is apt to get into a chaos of thinkingness or creatingness or livingness.

You can look at any eccentric or aberrated person and discover rapidly, by an inspection of him, which one of these four factors he is violating. He either is unable to know or not-know his own created thoughts, or he is unable to know or not-know the thoughts of others. Somewhere, for some reason best known to him, in his anxiety to be part of the game, he has shelved, lost, one of these abilities.

Time is a process of knowing in the present and not-knowing in the future or the past. Remembering is the process of knowing the past; prediction is the process of knowing the future. Forgetting is the process of not-knowing the past, and living "only for today" is the process of not-knowing the future.

Exercises in these various items rehabilitate not only the sanity or ability of the individual, but his general capability in living and playing the game.

10

The Goal of Scientology

10

The
Goal of
Scientology

The end object of Scientology is not the making into nothing of all of existence or the freeing of the individual of any and all traps everywhere. The goal of Scientology is making the individual capable of living a better life in his own estimation and with his fellows, and the playing of a better game.

11

Scientology Processing

11

Scientology Processing

Scientology is applied in many ways to many fields. One particular and specialized method of application of Scientology is its use on individuals and groups of people in the eradication of physical problems deriving from mental states and the improvement of their abilities and intelligence. By *processing* is meant the verbal exercising of an individual (preclear) in exact Scientology processes. There is a great deal of terminology and precision in these processes and their use, and they are not combinable with older mental activities such as psychiatry, psychology, psychoanalysis, yoga, massage, etc. However, these processes are capable of addressing or treating the same ills of the mind as are delineated by older methodology, with the addition that Scientology is alone in its ability to successfully eradicate those psychosomatic problems to which it is addressed. It is the only science or study known which is capable of uniformly producing marked and significant increases in intelligence and general ability.

Scientology processing, among other things, can improve the intelligence quotient[1] of an individual, his ability or desire to

---

1. **intelligence quotient:** a number indicating a person's level of intelligence.

communicate, his social attitudes, his capability and domestic harmony, his fertility, his artistic creativity, his reaction time and his health.

An additional sphere of activity allied to processing is Preventive Scientology. In this branch of processing, an individual is inhibited or restrained from assuming states lower than he has already suffered from. In other words, the progress of tendencies, neuroses, habits and deteriorating activities can be halted by Scientology or their occurrence can be prevented. This is done by processing the individual on standard Scientology processes without particular attention to the disability involved.

Scientology processing is called *auditing,* by which the auditor "listens, computes and commands." The auditor and the preclear are together out-of-doors or in a quiet place where they will not be disturbed or where they are not being subjected to interrupting influences. The purpose of the auditor is to give the preclear certain and exact commands which the preclear can follow and perform. The purpose of the auditor is to increase the ability of the preclear. The Auditor's Code is the governing set of rules for the general activity of auditing. The code follows:

The Auditor's Code

1. Do not evaluate[2] for the preclear.
2. Do not invalidate[3] or correct the preclear's data.
3. Use the processes which improve the preclear's case.
4. Keep all appointments once made.
5. Do not process a preclear after 10 P.M.

---

2. **evaluate:** tell the preclear what to think about his case.

3. **invalidate:** refute, degrade, discredit or deny something someone else considers to be fact.

6. Do not process a preclear who is improperly fed or who has not received enough rest.
7. Do not permit a frequent change of auditors.
8. Do not sympathize with the preclear.
9. Never permit the preclear to end the session on his own independent decision.
10. Never walk off from a preclear during a session.
11. Never get angry with a preclear.
12. Always reduce every communication lag[4] encountered by continued use of the same question or process.
13. Always continue a process as long as it produces change and no longer.
14. Be willing to grant beingness to the preclear.
15. Never mix the processes of Scientology with those of various other practices.
16. Always remain in good two-way communication[5] with the preclear during sessions.
17. Never use Scientology to obtain personal and unusual favors or unusual compliance from the preclear for the auditor's own personal profit.
18. Estimate the current case of your preclear with reality and do not audit another imagined case.
19. Do not explain, justify or make excuses for any auditor mistakes whether real or imagined.

---

4. **communication lag:** the length of time intervening between the asking of the question by the auditor and the reply to that specific question by the preclear. The question must be precise; the reply must be precisely to that question. It does not matter what intervenes in the time between the asking of the question and the receipt of the answer. The preclear may outflow, jabber, discuss, pause, hedge, disperse, dither or be silent; no matter what he does or how he does it, between the asking of the question and the giving of the answer, the *time* is the communication lag.

5. **two-way communication:** a normal cycle of a communication between two people. A two-way cycle of communication would work as follows: Joe, having originated a communication, and having completed it, may then wait for Bill to originate a communication to Joe, thus completing the remainder of the two-way cycle.

The Auditor's Code governs the activity of the auditor during sessions. The activity of the Scientologist in general is governed by another broader code.

The Code of a Scientologist

As a Scientologist, I pledge myself to the Code of a Scientologist for the good of all:

1. To keep Scientologists, the public and the press accurately informed concerning Scientology, the world of mental health and society.

2. To use the best I know of Scientology to the best of my ability to help my family, friends, groups and the world.

3. To refuse to accept for processing and to refuse to accept money from any preclear or group I feel I cannot honestly help.

4. To decry and do all I can to abolish any and all abuses against life and mankind.

5. To expose and help abolish any and all physically damaging practices in the field of mental health.

6. To help clean up and keep clean the field of mental health.

7. To bring about an atmosphere of safety and security in the field of mental health by eradicating its abuses and brutality.

8. To support true humanitarian endeavors in the fields of human rights.

9. To embrace the policy of equal justice for all.

10. To work for freedom of speech in the world.

11. To actively decry the suppression of knowledge, wisdom, philosophy or data which would help mankind.

12. To support the freedom of religion.

13. To help Scientology organizations and groups ally themselves with public groups.

14. To teach Scientology at a level it can be understood and used by the recipients.

15. To stress the freedom to use Scientology as a philosophy in all its applications and variations in the humanities.

16. To insist upon standard and unvaried Scientology as an applied activity in ethics,[6] processing and administration in Scientology organizations.

17. To take my share of responsibility for the impact of Scientology upon the world.

18. To increase the numbers and strength of Scientology over the world.

19. To set an example of the effectiveness and wisdom of Scientology.

20. To make this world a saner, better place.

As it can be seen, both of these codes are designed to protect the preclear as well as Scientology and the auditor in general. As these codes evolve from many years of observation and experience by a great number of people, it can be said that they are intensely important and are probably complete. Failure to observe them has resulted in a failure of Scientology. Scientology can do what it can do only when it is used within the limits of these two codes. Thus it can be seen that the interjection of peculiarities or practices by the auditor into Scientology processing can actually nullify and eradicate the benefits of that processing. Any hope or promise in Scientology is conditional upon its good use by the individual and its use in particular within the limits of these two codes.

---

6. **ethics:** the actions a person takes on himself. Ethics have to do with the code of agreement amongst people that they will conduct themselves in a fashion which will attain to the optimum solution to their problems.

The Conditions of Auditing

Certain definite conditions must prevail and a certain methodology must be followed in order that processing may be beneficial to its fullest extent.

Probably the first condition is a good grasp of Scientology as a science and its mission in the world.

The second condition would be a relaxed state of mind on the part of the auditor and the confidence that his use of Scientology upon the preclear will not produce a harmful result.

The third requisite should be finding a preclear. By this it is literally meant that one should discover somebody willing to be processed, and, having discovered one so willing, should then make sure that he is aware that he is there being processed.

The fourth requisite would be a quiet place in which to audit, with every precaution taken that the preclear will not be interrupted or burst in upon or unduly startled during processing.

12

Exact Processes

12

Exact
Processes

Auditing
Game and No-Game Conditions

In Scientology, the most important single elements to the auditor are *game conditions*[1] and *no-game conditions*. Reason—all games are aberrative.

All processing is directed toward establishing game conditions. Little or no processing is directed toward no-game conditions. Therefore, it is of the utmost importance to know exactly what these are, for one could be superficial about it and lose.

Rule—all games are aberrative, some are fun.

The elements of games to the auditor are:

---

1. **game conditions:** the factors which make a game, which is a contest of person against person or team against team. A game consists of freedoms, barriers and purposes, and there is a necessity in a game to have an opponent or an enemy. Also, there is a necessity to have problems, and enough individuality to cope with a situation. To live life fully, then, one must have, in addition to "something to do," a higher purpose; and this purpose, to be a purpose at all, must have counter-purposes or purposes which prevent it from occurring. If a person lacks problems, opponents and counter-purposes to his own, he will invent them. Here we have in essence the totality of aberration.

A game consists of freedoms, barriers and purposes.

In a game one's own team or self must receive no-effect and must deliver an effect upon the other team or opponent.

A game should have space and, preferably, a playing field.

A game is played in the same time continuum[2] for both sides (all players).

A game must have something which one does not have in order for it to be won.

Some part of the dynamics must be excluded for a game condition to exist. The amount of the dynamics excluded represents the tone of the game.

Games occur only when there is intention opposing intention, purpose opposing purpose.

A scarcity of games forces the preclear to accept less desirable games.

Participation in any game (whether it be the game of sick man, jealous wife or polo) is preferable to being in a no-game condition.

The type of game entered by a person is determined by his consideration as to how much and what kind of an effect he may receive while trying to deliver an effect.

---

2. **continuum:** a continuous whole, quantity or series; things whose parts cannot be separated or separately discerned.

Games are the basic mechanism for continuing attention.

To play a game one must be able to not-know his past and future and not-know his opponent's complete intentions.

Game conditions are:

Attention

Identity

Effect on opponents

No-effect on self

Can't have[3] on

   opponents and goals

   and their areas

Have on self,

   tools of play,

   own goals and field

Purpose

Problems of play

Self-determinism

Opponents

The possibility of loss

The possibility of

   winning

Communication

Non-arrival

No-game conditions are:

Knowing all

Not-knowing everything

Serenity

Namelessness

No-effect on opponent

Effect on self or team

Others have everything

Self can't have

Solutions

Pan-determinism

Friendship with all

Understanding

Total communication

No-communication

Win

Lose

No universe

No playing field

Arrival

Death

---

3. **can't have:** a depriving of self or others of substance or action or things.

Process only with those conditions listed as game conditions. Do not process directly toward those conditions listed as no-game conditions. So doing, the auditor will run out (erase) the aberrative effect of games and restore an ability to play a game.

Identities — Valences

There are four identities or valences.

When one is in his "own" valence he is said to be "himself."

As he departs from his own identity he comes into the following:

Exchanged Valence: One has directly superimposed the identity of another on his own. Example—Daughter becomes own mother to some degree. Remedy—One directly runs out Mother.

Attention Valence: One has become the valence B because one wants attention from C. Example—One becomes Mother because Mother received attention from Father while self did not. Remedy—Run out Father even though preclear appears in valence of Mother.

Synthetic Valence: One takes a valence about which he has been told. Example—Mother tells child false things about Father, accuses child of being like Father, with result that child is forced into Father's valence. Remedy—Run out Mother even though preclear does not seem to be near Mother's valence.

Auditing Procedures

All requisites for auditing from here on are entirely concerned with procedures and processes. By auditing procedure is meant the general model of how one goes about addressing a preclear. This includes an ability to place one question worded exactly the same way over and over again to the preclear no matter how many times the preclear has answered the question. It should include the ability to acknowledge with a "good" and "all right" every time a preclear executes or completes the execution of a command. It should include the ability to accept a communication from the preclear. When the preclear has something to say, the auditor should acknowledge the fact that he has received the preclear's communication and should pay some attention to the communication.

Procedure also includes the ability to sense when the preclear is being overstrained by processing or is being unduly annoyed and to handle such crises in the session to prevent the preclear from leaving. An auditor should also have the ability of handling startling remarks or occurrences by the preclear. An auditor should also have the knack of preventing the preclear from talking obsessively[4] since prolonged conversation markedly reduces the havingness of the preclear, and the sooner long dissertations by the preclear are cut off the better for the session in general.

Processes as distinct from procedures consist of utilizing the principle of the gradient scale to the end of placing the preclear in better control of himself, his mind, the people and the universe around him.

By *gradient scale* is meant a proceeding from simplicity

---

4. **obsessively:** in a manner as if driven by a persistent urge a person cannot control.

toward greater difficulty, giving the preclear always no more than he can do, but giving him as much as he can do until he can handle a great deal. The idea here is to give the preclear nothing but wins and to refrain from giving the preclear losses in the game of processing. Thus it can be seen that processing is a team activity and is not itself a game whereby the auditor opposes and seeks to defeat the preclear and the preclear seeks to defeat the auditor, for when this condition exists little results in processing.

The earliest stage of auditing consists[5] in taking over control of the preclear so as to restore to the preclear more control of himself than he has had. The most fundamental step is, then, location, whereby the preclear is made to be aware of the fact that he is in an auditing room, that an auditor is present and that the preclear is being a preclear.

Those conditions will become quite apparent if one realizes that it would be very difficult for a son to process a father. A father is not likely to recognize anything else than the boy he raised in his auditor. Therefore, the father would have to be made aware of the fact that the son was a competent practitioner before the father could be placed under control in processing. One of the most elementary commands in Scientology is "Look at me, who am I?" After a preclear has been asked to do this many times until he can do so quickly and accurately and without protest, it can be said that the preclear will have "found" the auditor.

The preclear is asked by the auditor to control, which is to say, start, change and stop (the anatomy of control) anything he is capable of controlling. In a very bad case this might be a very small object being pushed around on a table, being started and changed and stopped each time specifically and only at the

---

5. **consists:** contains or is inherent (in something) as a cause, effect or characteristic.

auditor's command until the preclear himself realizes that he himself can start, change and stop the object. Sometimes four or five hours spent in this exercise are very well spent on a very difficult preclear.

The preclear is then asked to start, change and stop his own body under the auditor's specific and precise direction. In all of his commands the auditor must be careful never to give a second command before the first one has been fully obeyed. A preclear in this procedure is walked around the room and is made to start, change the direction of and stop his body, one of these at a time in emphasis, until he realizes that he can do so with ease. Only now could it be said that a session is well in progress or that a preclear is securely under the auditor's command.

It should be noted especially that the goal of Scientology is better self-determinism for the preclear. This rules out at once hypnotism, drugs, alcohol or other control mechanisms used by other and older therapies. It will be found that such things are not only not necessary, but they are in direct opposition to the goals of greater ability for the preclear.

The principal points of concentration for the auditor now become the ability of the preclear to have, the ability of the preclear to not-know and the ability of the preclear to play a game.

An additional factor is the ability of the preclear to be himself and not a number of other people, such as his father, his mother, his marital partner or his children.

The ability of the preclear is increased by addressing to him the process known as the Trio. These are three questions, or rather commands.

1. "Look around here and tell me what you could have."

2. "Look around here and tell me what you would permit to remain in place."

3. "Look around and tell me with what you could dispense."

Number 1 above is used usually about ten times, then Number 2 is used five times, and Number 3 is used once. This ratio of ten, five and one would be an ordinary or routine approach to havingness. The end in view is to bring the preclear into a condition whereby he can possess or own or have whatever he sees, without further conditions, ramifications[6] or restrictions. This is the most therapeutic of all processes, elementary as it might seem. It is done without too much two-way communication or discussion with the preclear, and it is done until the preclear can answer questions 1, 2 and 3 equally well. It should be noted at once that twenty-five hours of use of this process by an auditor upon a preclear brings about a very high rise in tone. By saying twenty-five hours, it is intended to give the idea of the length of time the process should be used. As it is a strain on the usual person to repeat the same question over and over, it will be seen that an auditor should be well disciplined or very well trained before he audits.

In the case of a preclear who is very unable, "can't have" is substituted for "have," etc., in each of the above questions for a few hours, until the preclear is ready for the Trio in its "have" form. This can–can't is the plus and minus aspect of all thought and in Scientology is called by a specialized word, *dichotomy*.

---

6. **ramifications:** related or derived subjects, problems, etc.; outgrowths; consequences.

The rehabilitation of the ability of the preclear to not-know is also rehabilitation of the preclear in the time stream since the process of time consists of knowing the moment and not-knowing the past and not-knowing the future simultaneously. This process, like all other Scientology processes, is repetitive. The process is run, ordinarily, only after the preclear is in very good condition and is generally run in an exterior, well-inhabited place. Here the auditor, without exciting public comment, indicates a person and asks the preclear, "Can you not-know something about that person?" The auditor does not permit the preclear to "not-know" things which the preclear already doesn't know. The preclear "not-knows" only those things which are visible and apparent about the person. This is also run on other objects in the environment such as walls, floors, chairs and other things. The auditor should not be startled when, for the preclear, large chunks of the environment start to disappear. This is ordinary routine and, in effect, the preclear should make the entirety of the environment disappear at his own command. The environment does not disappear for the auditor. The end goal of this "not-know" process is the disappearance of the entire universe, under the preclear's control, but only for the preclear.

It will be discovered while running this that the preclear's "havingness" may deteriorate. If this happens, he was not run enough on the Trio before he was run on this process. It is only necessary in such a case to intersperse "Look around here and tell me what you could have" with the "not-know" command to keep the preclear in good condition. Drop of havingness is manifested by nervous agitation, obsessive talk or semi-unconsciousness or "dopiness" on the part of the preclear. These manifestations indicate only reduction of havingness.

The reverse of the question here is "Tell me something that you would be willing to have that person (indicated by the auditor) not-know about you." Both sides of the question have to be run (audited). This process can be continued for twenty-five hours or even fifty or seventy-five hours of auditing with considerable benefit so long as it does not react too violently upon the preclear in terms of loss of havingness.

It should be noted that, in running either havingness or "not-know" on a preclear, the preclear may "exteriorize." In other words, it may become apparent, either by his observation or because the preclear informs him, that the auditor has "exteriorized" a preclear. Under "The Parts of Man" section there is an explanation of this phenomenon. In modern auditing the auditor does not do anything odd about this beyond receive and be interested in the preclear's statement of the fact. The preclear should not be permitted to become alarmed since it is a usual manifestation. A preclear is in better condition and will audit better exteriorized than "in his head."

Understanding that an actual ability to "not-know" is an ability to erase, by self-command, the past, without suppressing it with energy or going into any other method, is necessary to help the preclear. It is the primary rehabilitation in terms of knowingness. Forgetting is a lower manifestation than "not-knowingness."

The third ability to be addressed by the auditor is the ability of the preclear to play a game. First and foremost in the requisites to playing a game is the ability to control. One must be able to control something in order to participate in a game. Therefore the general rehabilitation of control by starting, changing and stopping things is a rehabilitation in the ability to play a game. When a preclear refuses to recover, it is because the preclear is using his state as a game, and does not believe that there is any better game for him to play than the state he is in. He may protest if this is called a game. Nevertheless, any condition will surrender if the auditor has the preclear invent similar conditions or even tell lies about the existing condition. Inventing games or inventing conditions or inventing problems alike rehabilitate the ability to play a game. Chief among these various rehabilitation factors are control (start, change and stop), problems and the willingness to overwhelm or be overwhelmed. One ceases to be able to have games when one loses control over various things, when one becomes short of problems and when one is unwilling to be overwhelmed (in other words, to lose) or to overwhelm (to win). It will be found while running havingness as in the Trio above that one may run down the ability to play a game, since havingness is the reward of a game in part.

In the matter of problems it will be seen that these are completely necessary to the playing of a game. The anatomy of a problem is intention versus intention. This is, of course, in essence the purpose of all games, to have two sides, each one with an opposed intention. Technically a problem is two or more purposes in conflict. It is very simple to detect whether or not the preclear is suffering from a scarcity of games. The preclear who needs more games clutches to himself various present time problems.[7] If an auditor is confronted with a preclear who is being obsessed by a problem in present time he knows two things: (1) that the preclear's ability to play a game is low, and (2) that he must run an exact process at once to rehabilitate the preclear in session.

It often happens at the beginning of an auditing session that the preclear has encountered a heavy present time problem between sessions. The preclear must always be consulted before the session is actually in progress as to whether or not he has "anything worrying" him. To a preclear who is worried about

---

7. **present time problems:** special problems that exist in the physical universe now, on which the preclear has his attention fixed. Any sets of circumstances that so engage the attention of the preclear that he feels he should be doing something about it instead of being audited.

some present time situation or problem no other process has any greater effectiveness than the following one. The auditor with a very *brief* discussion of the problem asks the preclear to invent a problem of comparable magnitude. He may have to reword this request to make the preclear understand it completely, but the auditor wants, in essence, the preclear to invent or create a problem he considers similar to the problem he has. If the preclear is unable to do this, it is necessary, then, to have him lie about the problem which he has. Lying is the lowest order of creativeness. After he has lied about the problem for a short time, it will be found that he will be able to invent problems. He should be made to invent problem after problem until he is no longer concerned with his present time problem.

The auditor should understand that a preclear who is "now willing to do something about the problem" has not been run long enough on the invention of problems of comparable magnitude. As long as the preclear is attempting to *do* something about the problem, the problem is still of obsessive importance to him. No session can be continued successfully until such a present time problem is entirely flat,[8] and it has been the experience, when a present time problem is not completely eradicated by this process, that the remainder of the session or indeed the entire course of auditing may be interrupted.

When a preclear does not seem to be advancing under auditing, a thing which he does markedly and observedly, it must then be supposed that the preclear has a present time problem which has not been eradicated and which must be handled in auditing. Although the auditor gives the preclear to understand that he too believes this present time problem is extremely important, the auditor should not believe that this

---

8. **flat:** discharged of all bad reactions to the preclear. No longer producing change or a reaction.

process will not handle *any* present time problem, since it will. This process should be done on some preclears in company with the Trio.

If the preclear is asked to "lie about" or "invent a problem of comparable magnitude," and while doing so becomes agitated or unconscious or begins to talk wildly or obsessively, it must be assumed that he will have to have some havingness run on him until the agitation or manifestation ceases so that the problem of comparable magnitude process can be resumed.

Another aspect of the ability to play a game is the willingness to win and the willingness to lose. An individual has to be willing to be cause or willing to be an effect. As far as games are concerned, this is reduced to a willingness to win and a willingness to lose. People become afraid of defeat and afraid of failure. The entire anatomy of failure is only that one's postulates or intentions are reversed in action. For instance, one intends to strike a wall and strikes it. That is a win. One intends not to strike a wall and doesn't strike it. That is again a win. One intends not to strike a wall and strikes it. That is a lose. One intends to strike a wall and can't strike it. This is again a lose. It will be seen in this as well as other things that the most significant therapy there is, is changing the mind. All things are as one considers they are and no other way. If it is sufficiently simple to give the definition of winning and losing, so it is simple to process the matter.

This condition is best expressed, it appears, in processing by a process known as "Overwhelming." An elementary way of running this is to take the preclear outside where there are numbers of people to observe and, indicating a person, to ask the preclear, "What could overwhelm that person?" When the preclear answers this, he is asked about the same person, "What could that person overwhelm?" He is then asked as the third question, "Look around here and tell me what you could have." These three questions are run one after the other. Then another person is chosen and then the three questions are asked again.

This process can be varied in its wording, but the central idea must remain as above. The preclear can be asked, "What would you permit to overwhelm that person?" and "What would you permit that person to overwhelm?" and of course, "Look around here and tell me what you could have." This is only one of a number of possible processes on the subject of overwhelming, but it should be noted that asking the preclear to think of things which would overwhelm *him* could be fatal to the case. Where overwhelming is handled, the preclear should be given a detached view.

A counter-position to havingness processes, but one which is less therapeutic, is "Separateness." One asks the preclear to "Look around and discover things which are separate from things." This is repeated over and over. It is, however, destructive of havingness even though it will occasionally prove beneficial.

It will be seen that havingness (barriers), "not-knowingness" (being in present time and not in the past or the future), purposes (problems, antagonists or intention–counter-intention) and separateness (freedom) will cover the anatomy of games. It is not to be thought, however, that havingness addresses itself only to games. Many other factors enter into it. In among all of these, it is of the greatest single importance.

One addresses, in these days of Scientology, the subjective self, the mind, as little as possible. One keeps the preclear alert to the broad environment around him. An address to the various energy patterns of the mind is less beneficial than exercises which directly approach other people or the physical universe.

Therefore, asking a preclear to sit still and answer the question "What could you have?" when it is answered by the preclear from his experience or on the score of things which are not present, is found to be nontherapeutic and is found instead to decrease the ability and intelligence of the preclear. This is what is known as a *subjective*[9] process.

These are the principal processes which produce marked gains. There are other processes and there are combinations of processes, but these given here are the most important. A Scientologist knowing the mind completely can of course do many "tricks" with the conditions of people to improve them. One of these is the ability to address a psychosomatic illness such as a crippled leg which, having nothing physically wrong with it, yet is not usable. The auditor could ask the preclear, "Tell me a lie about your leg," with a possible relief of the pain or symptoms. Asking the preclear repeatedly, "Look around here and tell me something your leg could have," would undoubtedly release the somatic. Asking the preclear with the bad leg, "What problem could your leg be to you?" or desiring him to "Invent a problem of comparable magnitude to your leg," would produce a distinct change in the condition of the leg. This would apply to any other body part or organ. It would also apply, strangely enough, to the preclear's possessions. If a preclear had a vehicle or cart which was out of repair or troublesome to him, one could ask him "What problem could a cart be to you?" and thus, requesting him to invent many such problems, one would discover that he had solved his problems with the cart.

There is the phenomenon in existence that the preclear already has many set games. When one asks him to give the

9. **subjective:** proceeding from or taking place in an individual's mind.

auditor problems, he already has the manifestations of as-ising[10] or erasing taking place. Thought erases; therefore, the number of problems or games the preclear could have would be reduced by asking him to recount[11] those which he already has. Asking the preclear to describe his symptoms is far less than therapeutic and may result in a worsening of those symptoms, contrary to what some schools of thought have believed in the past but which accounts for their failures.

There are specific things which one must avoid in auditing. These follow:

1. *Significances.*[12] The easiest thing a thetan does is change his mind. The most difficult thing he does is handle the environment in which he finds himself situated. Therefore, asking a thetan to run out various ideas is a fallacy.[13] It is a mistake. Asking the preclear to think over something can also be an error. Asking a preclear to do exercises which concern his mind alone can be entirely fatal. A preclear is processed between himself and his environment. If he is processed between himself and his mind, he is processed up too short a view and his condition will worsen.

2. *Two-way communication.* There can be far too much two-way communication or far too much communication in an auditing session. Communication involves the reduction of havingness. Letting a preclear talk on and on or obsessively

---

10. **as-ising:** viewing anything exactly as it is without any distortions or lies, at which moment it will vanish and cease to exist.

11. **recount:** to tell in detail; give the facts or particulars of.

12. **significances:** a word which is used in the special sense to denote any thoughts, decisions, concepts, ideas or meanings in the mind in distinction to its masses. (The mind is basically composed of masses and significances.)

13. **fallacy:** a delusive (misleading, deceptive) notion, especially one based on false reasoning.

is to let a preclear reduce his havingness. The preclear who is permitted to go on talking will talk himself down tone scale and into a bad condition. It is better for the auditor simply and discourteously to tell a preclear to "shut up" than to have the preclear run himself "out of the bottom" on havingness. You can observe this for yourself. If you permit a person, who is not too able, to talk about his troubles and to keep on talking, he will begin to talk more and more hectically.[14] He is reducing his havingness. He will eventually talk himself down the tone scale into apathy at which time he will be willing to tell you (as you insist upon it) that he "feels better" when, as a matter of fact, he is actually worse. Asking a preclear, "How do you feel now?" can reduce his havingness since he looks over his present time condition and as-ises some mass.

3. *Too many processes.* It is possible to run a preclear on too many processes in too short a time with a reduction of the preclear's recovery. This is handled by observing the communication lag of the preclear. It will be discovered that the preclear will space his answers to a repeated question differently with each answer. When a long period ensues between the question and his answer to the question a second time, he is said to have a *communication lag*. The *communication lag* is the length of time between the placing of the question by the auditor and the answering of that *exact* question by the preclear. It is not the length of time between the placing of the question by the auditor and some statement by the preclear.

It will be found that the communication lag lengthens and shortens on a repeated question. The question on the tenth

---

14. **hectically:** in a manner characterized by intense agitation, excitement, confused and rapid movement.

---

time it has been asked may detect no significant lag. This is the time to stop asking that question since it now has no appreciable communication lag. One can leave any process when the communication lag for three successive questions is the same.

In order to get from one process to another, one employs a communication bridge[15] which to a marked degree reduces the liability of too many processes. A communication bridge is always used.

Before a question is asked, the preclear should have the question discussed with him and the wording of the question agreed upon, as though he were making a contract with the auditor. The auditor says that he is going to have the preclear do certain things and finds out if it's all right with the preclear if the auditor asks him to do these things. This is the first part of a communication bridge. It precedes all questions, but when one is changing from one process to another the bridge becomes a bridge indeed. One levels out the old process by asking the preclear whether or not he doesn't think it is safe to leave that process now. One discusses the possible benefit received from the process and then tells the preclear that he is no longer going to use that process. Now he tells the preclear he is going to use a new process, describes the process and gets an agreement on it. When the agreement is achieved, then he uses this process. The communication bridge is used at all times. The last half of it, the agreement on a new process, is used always before any process is begun.

---

15. **communication bridge:** an auditing procedure which closes off the process one is running, maintains ARC, and opens up the new process on which one is about to embark. It is used so that a pc will not be startled by change, for if one changes too rapidly in a session, one sticks the preclear in the session every time. He is given some warning, and that is what a communication bridge is for.

4. *Failure to handle the present time problem.* Probably more cases are stalled or found unable to benefit in processing because of the neglect of the present time problem, as covered above, than any other single item.

5. *Unconsciousness, "dopiness" or agitation on the part of the preclear* is not a mark of good condition. It is a loss of havingness. The preclear must never be processed into unconsciousness or "dopiness." He should always be kept alert. The basic phenomenon of unconsciousness is "a flow which has flowed too long in one direction." If one talks too long at somebody he will render him unconscious. In order to wake up the target of all that talk, it is necessary to get the unconscious person to do some talking. It is simply necessary to reverse any flow to make unconsciousness disappear, but this is normally cared for in modern Scientology by running the Trio above.

The Future of Scientology

With man now equipped with weapons sufficient to destroy all mankind on Earth, the emergence of a new science capable of handling man is vital. Scientology is such a science. It was born in the same crucible[16] as the atomic bomb. The basic intelligence of Scientology came from nuclear physics, higher mathematics and the understanding of the ancients in the East. Scientology can and does do exactly what it says it can do. In Washington, DC, there is an enormous file cabinet filled with thousands of case histories, fully validated and sworn to, which attest the scientific thoroughness of Scientology. With Scientology man can prevent insanity, criminality and war. It is for man to use. It is for the betterment of man. The primary race of Earth is not between one nation and another today. The only race that matters at this

---

16. **crucible:** a severe, searching test.

moment is the one being run between Scientology and the atomic bomb. The history of man, as has been said by well-known authorities, may well depend upon which one wins.

Finis

Appendix

The Aims
of Scientology

A civilization without insanity, without criminals and without war, where the able can prosper and honest beings can have rights, and where man is free to rise to greater heights, are the aims of Scientology.

First announced to an enturbulated world fifteen years ago, these aims are well within the grasp of our technology.

Nonpolitical in nature, Scientology welcomes any individual of any creed,[1] race or nation.

We seek no revolution. We seek only evolution to higher states of being for the individual and for society.

We are achieving our aims.

After endless millennia[2] of ignorance about himself, his mind and the universe, a breakthrough has been made for man.

---

1. **creed:** any system, doctrine or formula of religious belief.
2. **millennia:** periods of one thousand years.

Other efforts man has made have been surpassed.

The combined truths of fifty thousand years of thinking men, distilled and amplified by new discoveries about man, have made for this success.

We welcome you to Scientology. We only expect of you your help in achieving our aims and helping others. We expect you to be helped.

Scientology is the most vital movement on Earth today.

In a turbulent world, the job is not easy. But then, if it were, we wouldn't have to be doing it.

We respect man and believe he is worthy of help. We respect you and believe you, too, can help.

Scientology does not owe its help. We have done nothing to cause us to propitiate.[3] Had we done so, we would not now be bright enough to do what we are doing.

Man suspects all offers of help. He has often been betrayed, his confidence shattered. Too frequently he has given his trust and been betrayed. We may err, for we build a world with broken straws. But we will never betray your faith in us so long as you are one of us.

The sun never sets on Scientology.

And may a new day dawn for you, for those you love and for man.

---

3. **propitiate:** act in a manner calculated to reduce the anger or win the favor of another; try to make calm or quiet.

Our aims are simple, if great.

And we will succeed, and are succeeding at each new revolution of the Earth.

Your help is acceptable to us.

Our help is yours.

L. Ron Hubbard
September, 1965

About the Author

L. Ron Hubbard is acclaimed by millions as the foremost author of self-betterment books in the world today, primarily because his writing expresses a firsthand knowledge of the nature of man—a knowledge gained not from standing on the sidelines but from personally experiencing every aspect of life.

"To really know life, you've got to be a part of life," Ron said. "You must get down and look; you must get into the nooks and crannies of existence; you have to rub elbows with all kinds of men before you can finally establish what man is."

He did exactly that. As a young man traveling the world, he observed firsthand a multitude of cultures and races. He talked and listened to people—all kinds of people in every imaginable life situation. He never was nor would he ever be an ivory-tower philosopher.

By the time he was nineteen he had traveled a quarter of a million miles, including voyages to China, Japan and other points in the Orient and South Pacific, and had become intimately familiar with Eastern cultures, beliefs and philosophies. But he was by no means a stranger to modern Western thought. He studied engineering at George Washington University and while there attended one of the first American classes ever taught on nuclear physics.

Ron's travels, his formal studies and his own observations convinced him that there was no workable technology of the human mind and that the mental "technologies" which had been evolved on this planet were in fact barbarisms.

Determined to remedy this, he devoted his life to extensive research into the mysteries of the mind and life itself. His work first came into broad public view in May 1950, with the publication of *Dianetics: The Modern Science of Mental Health*. This book exploded onto the world scene and immediately became a bestseller and has continued to be immensely popular with people from all walks of life to this day. The reason is simple: His guiding principle was always workability, and Dianetics *works*.

Ron continued his studies, which led him further and further into the realm of the human spirit. Breakthrough after breakthrough followed, each pushing aside previously insurmountable barriers and opening up new vistas of existence. These advances were codified and became the principal tenets of Scientology, a workable way to improve life in this troubled world.

In 1956, Ron wrote *Scientology: The Fundamentals of Thought* as an introduction to basic Scientology principles for people new to the subject. With the publishing of this book he made it possible for anyone to gain an extremely useful insight into life, and then use that knowledge to better conditions for himself and his friends.

Over the next three decades of his life he continued his activities of helping others and developing the route to a higher level of understanding which could be traveled by anyone.

His works—including an astounding number of books, taped lectures, writings, instructional films, demonstrations, briefings, all delineating Scientology and Dianetics technology and its application—are studied and applied by people on every continent across the world. There are now hundreds of Scientology and Dianetics organizations spanning the globe and millions of individuals using this technology daily to effectively improve their lives.

With his discoveries and writings, Ron created and made known the knowledge and technology necessary to change the face of civilization on Earth. As Ron summates in this book, "With Scientology man can prevent insanity, criminality and war. It is for man to use. It is for the betterment of man. The primary race of Earth is not between one nation and another today. The only race that matters at this moment is the one being run between Scientology and the atomic bomb. The history of man, as has been said by well-known authorities, may well depend upon which one wins."

With his research fully completed, L. Ron Hubbard departed his body on 24 January 1986.

He has mapped the route to total freedom and made it available to all.

Millions of people all over the world consider they have no truer friend.

—The Editors

Glossary

Aberration: a departure from rational thought or behavior. From the Latin, *aberrare*, to wander from; Latin, *ab*, away, *errare*, to wander. It means basically to err, to make mistakes, or more specifically, to have fixed ideas which are not true. The word is also used in its scientific sense. It means departure from a straight line. If a line should go from A to B and it is "aberrated," it would go from A to some other point, to some other point, to some other point, to some other point, to some other point and finally arrive at B. Taken in its scientific sense, it would also mean the lack of straightness or to see crookedly as, for example, a man sees a horse but thinks he sees an elephant. Aberrated conduct would be wrong conduct, or conduct not supported by reason. Aberration is opposed to sanity, which would be its opposite.

adjoining: being in contact at some point or line; located next to another; bordering.

aggrandize: to make greater, more powerful, richer, etc.

analytical mind: the conscious, aware mind which thinks, observes data, remembers it and resolves problems. It would be essentially the conscious mind as opposed to the unconscious mind.

anatomical: of or connected with the structure of an organism or body.

anchor points: points which demark (limit) the outermost boundaries of a space or its corners.

Anglo-American: belonging to, relating to or involving England and America, especially the United States, or the people of the two countries.

Aquinas, St. Thomas: (1225?–74) Italian religious philosopher.

ARC triangle: a triangle which is a symbol of the fact that affinity, reality and communication act together as a whole entity and that one of them cannot be considered unless the other two are also taken into account. Without affinity there is no reality or communication. Without reality or some agreement, affinity and communication are absent. Without communication there can be no affinity or reality. It is only necessary to improve one corner of this very valuable triangle in Scientology in order to improve the remaining two corners.

arrant: that is plainly such; out-and-out; notorious.

artifact: any object made by human beings, especially with a view to subsequent use.

as-ising: viewing anything exactly as it is without any distortions or lies, at which moment it will vanish and cease to exist.

ascendancy: position in which one has control or power; supremacy.

aspiration: strong desire or ambition.

assertive: confidently aggressive or self-assured.

assumption: the act of taking possession of something.

astral body: somebody's delusion. Astral bodies are usually mock-ups which the mystic then tries to believe real. He sees the astral body as something else and then seeks to inhabit it in the most common practices of "astral walking."

Attila: (406?–53) king of the Huns, a nomadic and warlike Asian people who invaded and controlled large parts of Eastern and Central Europe.

auditor: a person trained and qualified in applying Scientology procedures to individuals for their betterment; called an auditor because *auditor* means "one who listens."

authoritarian: favoring complete obedience to authority as opposed to individual freedom.

automaticity: something one is doing that he is not aware he is doing or is partially aware he is doing. Non-self-determined action which ought to be determined by the individual. The individual ought to be determining an action and he is not determining it.

axiom: statement of natural law on the order of those of the physical sciences.

basic personality: the individual himself. The basic individual is not a buried unknown or a different person, but an intensity of all that is best and most able in the person.

behold: observe; look at; see.

beingness: condition or state of being; existence.

between-lives area: the experiences of a thetan during the time between the loss of a body and the assumption of another.

biophysics: the branch of physics dealing with the way the laws of physics apply to living things.

black screens: parts of mental image pictures where the preclear is looking at blackness.

brigandage: plundering by brigands [bandits].

can't have: a depriving of self or others of substance or action or things.

cause-distance-effect: *See* **communication.**

cessation: stopping, either forever or for some time.

chemistry: the science dealing with the composition and properties of substances, and with the reactions by which substances are produced from or converted into other substances.

commodity: a thing of use.

common denominator: a characteristic, element, etc., held in common.

communication: the interchanges of ideas across space. Its fullest definition is the consideration and action of impelling an impulse or particle from source-point across a distance to receipt-point, with the intention of bringing into being at the receipt-point a duplication and understanding of that which emanated from the source-point. The formula of Communication is Cause, Distance, Effect, with Intention, Attention and Duplication with Understanding.

communication bridge: an auditing procedure which closes off the process one is running, maintains ARC, and opens up the new process on which one is about to embark. It is used so that a pc will not be startled by change, for if one changes too rapidly in a session, one sticks the preclear in the session every time. He is given some warning, and that is what a communication bridge is for.

communication lag: the length of time intervening between the asking of the question by the auditor and the reply to that specific question by the preclear. The question must be precise; the reply must be precisely to that question. It does not matter what intervenes in the time between the asking of the question and the receipt of the answer. The preclear may outflow, jabber, discuss, pause, hedge, disperse, dither or be silent; no matter what he does or how he does it, between the asking of the question and the giving of the answer, the *time* is the communication lag.

compulsively: in a manner as if compelled, urged, driven or forced.

concentric: having a center in common.

consists: contains or is inherent (in something) as a cause, effect or characteristic.

construed: having a certain meaning placed on.

continuum: a continuous whole, quantity or series; things whose parts cannot be separated or separately discerned.

cravenness: condition of being very cowardly or afraid.

creed: any system, doctrine or formula of religious belief.

crucible: a severe, searching test.

cult: devoted attachment to, or extravagant admiration for, a person, principle, etc., especially when regarded as a fad.

decries: speaks out against strongly and openly; denounces.

derangement: condition of having been upset in arrangement, order or operation; unsettled; disordered.

Dianetics: man's most advanced school of the mind. The word comes from Greek *dia* (through) and *nous* (soul). Dianetics is defined as what the soul is doing to the body. It is a way of handling the energy of which life is made in such a way as to bring about a greater efficiency in the organism and in the spiritual life of the individual.

dialectical materialism: in logic, "dialectic" is the action and reaction between opposites, out of which a new synthesis (harmony of the two opposites) emerges. This was an idea originated by the German philosopher Georg Wilhelm Hegel (1770–1831). "Materialism" is a philosophy which falsely maintains that there is nothing in the universe but matter, that mind is a phenomenon of matter, and that there is no ground for assuming a spiritual first cause. "Dialectical materialism" was an adaption of these ideas by German revolutionary leader and founder of modern socialism Karl Marx (1818–83) into his own "general laws of motion which govern the evolution of nature and society." He held that a conflict of opposites in human society is the evolutionary process by which a classless society would eventually be reached.

dilettante: of or characteristic of a person who follows an art or science only for amusement and in a superficial way.

discourse: communication of ideas, information, etc., especially by talking; conversation.

disdains: thinks unworthy of notice, response, etc.; considers beneath oneself.

dissertation: a formal discussion of a subject.

dissuaded: turned aside (from a course, etc.) by persuasion or advice.

dwindling spiral: a phenomenon of the ARC triangle whereby when one breaks some affinity, a little bit of the reality goes down, and then communication goes down, which makes it impossible to get affinity as high as before; so a little bit more gets knocked off affinity, and then reality goes down, and then communication. This is the dwindling spiral in progress, until it hits the bottom—death—which is no affinity, no communication and no reality.

dynamics: there could be said to be eight urges (drives, impulses) in life. These we call dynamics. These are motives or motivations.

eccentricities: deviations from what is ordinary or customary, as in conduct or manner; oddities; unconventionalities.

equilateral: having all sides equal [an *equilateral* triangle].

ethics: the actions a person takes on himself. Ethics have to do with the code of agreement amongst people that they will conduct themselves in a fashion which will attain to the optimum solution to their problems.

euthanasia: the original definition of *euthanasia* is "mercy killing" or "easy death." However, under the practice of psychiatry it has become "the act of killing people considered a burden on society."

evaluate: tell the preclear what to think about his case.

evolutionaries: those concerned with evolution or development.

exploitation: making unethical use of for one's own advantage or profit.

expounded: explained or interpreted.

exteriorize: to bring about the state of the thetan, the individual himself, being outside his body. When this is done, the person achieves a certainty that he is himself and not his body.

factionalism: condition of conflict, discord or antagonism among members of a group.

fallacy: a delusive (misleading, deceptive) notion, especially one based on false reasoning.

flat: discharged of all bad reactions to the preclear. No longer producing change or a reaction.

flow: impulse or direction of thought, energy or action.

foundations: institutions financed by a donation or legacy to aid research, education, the arts, etc.

Frederick of Prussia: (1712–86) king of Prussia. Known as Frederick the Great, he conducted intermittent campaigns of conquest into neighboring countries. The wars he took his country into eventually involved all of Europe.

French Revolution: the revolution that began in France in 1789 with the overthrow of the French royal family and ended in 1799, with Napoleon's overthrow of the governing body established in 1795.

fruition: a coming to fulfillment; realization.

game conditions: the factors which make a game, which is a contest of person against person or team against team. A game consists of freedoms, barriers and purposes, and there is a necessity in a game to have an opponent or an enemy. Also, there is a necessity to have problems, and enough individuality to cope with a situation. To live life fully, then, one must have, in addition to "something to do," a higher purpose; and this purpose, to be a purpose at all, must have counter-purposes or purposes which prevent it from occurring. If a person lacks problems, opponents and counter-purposes to his own, he will invent them. Here we have in essence the totality of aberration.

Genghis Khan: (1162–1227) Mongol conqueror of much of Asia and Eastern Europe. His armies were totally ruthless in their actions and were said to have killed over a million people in one city alone.

germinate: to start developing or growing.

glandular: of, like or functioning as a gland (any organ or specialized group of cells that separates certain elements from the blood and secretes them in a form for the body to use or throw off).

guise: general external appearance.

harangue: to scold or address with a long or intense verbal attack.

hectically: in a manner characterized by intense agitation, excitement, confused and rapid movement.

Hitler, Adolf: (1889–1945) dictator of Germany from 1933 to 1945. In rising to power in Germany, he fortified his position through murder of real or imagined opponents and maintained police-state control over the population. He led Germany into World War II resulting in its nearly total destruction.

humanities: the branches of learning concerned with human thought and relations, as distinguished from the sciences.

ideology: the principal ideas or beliefs that characterize a particular class, group or movement.

immortal: not liable or subject to death; undying.

inculcate: to impress upon the mind by frequent repetition or persistent urging.

initiated: brought into practice or use; introduced; started.

intelligence quotient: a number indicating a person's level of intelligence.

interiorized: having gone into something and become a part of it too fixedly.

invalidate: refute, degrade, discredit or deny something someone else considers to be fact.

Kaiser Wilhelm: William II (1859–1941), emperor of Germany from 1888 to 1918. (*Kaiser* is German for "emperor.") Through inept handling of his power and authority as emperor, he helped cause the circumstances leading to World War I and thereby the deaths of millions of men on the battlefields.

keystone: something on which associated things depend.

knowingness: awareness not depending upon perception. One doesn't have to look to find out. For example, you do not have to get a perception or picture of where you are living to know where you live.

latterly: of late, nowadays.

mania: excessive excitement or enthusiasm.

manifest: readily perceived by the eye or the understanding; evident; obvious; apparent; plain.

Marxist: follower or believer in the doctrines of Karl Marx (1818–83), German political philosopher, regarded by some as the founder of modern socialism.

masses: compositions of matter and energy existing in the physical universe. Mental mass is contained in mental image pictures.

millennia: periods of one thousand years.

misorientation: wrong placing or positioning with regard to facts or principles.

mock-up: a knowingly created mental picture that is not part of the time track. It is a self-created image a person can see.

morose: ill-tempered; gloomy, sullen, etc.

mutation: change or alteration, as in form or nature.

Napoleon Bonaparte: (1769–1821) French military leader. He rose to power in France by military force, declared himself emperor and conducted campaigns of conquest across Europe until his final defeat by armies allied against him in 1815.

neurons: the structural and functional units of the nervous system.

neurosis: an obsession or compulsion that overmasters a person's self-determinism to such a degree that it is a social liability.

no-game condition: a totality of barriers or a totality of freedom. *See also* **game condition.**

obsessively: in a manner as if driven by a persistent urge a person cannot control.

obstetrics: the branch of medicine concerned with the care and treatment of women during pregnancy, childbirth and the period immediately following.

old saw: an old saying, often repeated; maxim; proverb.

orthopedics: the branch of surgery dealing with the treatment of deformities, diseases and injuries of the bones, joints, muscles, etc.

overwhelmed: overcome completely in mind or feeling.

palpable: clear to the mind; obvious; evident; plain.

panorama: a continuous series of scenes or events; constantly changing scene.

paramount: ranking higher than any other, as in power or importance; chief; supreme.

partisan: biased, prejudiced or one-sided.

party: a person or group that participates in some action, affair, plan, etc.; participant.

pastoral: of or involving the duties of a minister or priest in charge of a church.

patently: clearly; obviously; openly.

physics: the science dealing with the properties, changes and interactions, etc., of matter and energy.

postulate: to generate or think a concept. A concept is a thought, and to postulate infers a requirement that something *is* something or that it isn't something or that some action is going to take place. In other words, *postulate* infers conditions and actions rather than just plain thought. (Note to translators: Lacking a proper English word for "causative thinking," the word *postulate* has been used in slight difference to its English definition. If there is a word in your language which means "self-impulsion" or "creation of a thought," use that instead of *postulate*.)

practitioners: persons engaged in the practice of a profession, occupation, etc.

preclear: a person who, through Scientology processing, is finding out more about himself and life.

preposterous: so contrary to nature, reason or common sense as to be laughable; absurd; ridiculous.

present time problems: special problems that exist in the physical universe now, on which the preclear has his attention fixed. Any sets of circumstances that so engage the attention of the preclear that he feels he should be doing something about it instead of being audited.

processed: have Scientology processes and procedures applied to someone by a trained practitioner. Also called "audited."

processing: the application of Scientology processes and procedures to someone by a trained practitioner. The exact definition of auditing (processing) is: the action of asking a person a question (which he can understand and answer), getting an answer to that question and acknowledging him for that answer. Also called "auditing."

propitiate: act in a manner calculated to reduce the anger or win the favor of another; try to make calm or quiet.

psychoses: major forms of mental affliction or disease. A psychotic is an individual who cannot handle himself or his environment well enough to survive and who must be cared for to protect others from him or to protect him from himself.

psychosomatic: *psycho* refers to mind and *somatic* refers to body; the term *psychosomatic* means the mind making the body ill or illnesses which have been created physically within the body by derangement of the mind.

purveyors: providers or suppliers.

ramifications: related or derived subjects, problems, etc.; outgrowths; consequences.

randomities: things one picks out and agrees not to predict. Randomity is a consideration of motion. A person can have too much or too little motion, or enough motion. What is enough motion is measured by the consideration of the individual.

reactive mind: the portion of the mind which works on a stimulus-response basis (given a certain stimulus it will automatically give a certain response) which is not under a person's volitional control and which exerts force and power over a person's awareness, purposes, thoughts, body and actions.

recount: to tell in detail; give the facts or particulars of.

recourse: applying or going to for help, advice or information.

restimulation: the reactivation of a past memory due to similar circumstances in the present approximating circumstances of the past.

résumé: a summing up; summary.

Scientology: Scientology applied religious philosophy. It is the study and handling of the spirit in relationship to itself, universes and other life. Scientology means *scio,* knowing in the fullest sense of the word and *logos,* study. In itself the word means literally *knowing how to know.* Scientology is a "route," a way, rather than a dissertation or an assertive body of knowledge. Through its drills and studies one may find the truth for himself. The technology is therefore not expounded as something to believe, but something to *do.*

self-determinism: a condition of determining the actions of self. It is a first (self) dynamic action and leaves the remaining seven undetermined or, in actuality, in opposition to the self.

significances: a word which is used in a special sense to denote any thoughts, decisions, concepts, ideas or meanings in the mind in distinction to its masses. (The mind is basically composed of masses and significances.)

solvent: a dissolving or disintegrating influence.

somatic mind: that mind which takes care of the automatic mechanisms of the body, the regulation of the minutiae [precise details] which keep the organism running.

sovereignty: supreme and independent power or authority in government as possessed or claimed by a state or community.

statecraft: the art of government and diplomacy.

steerage: the act of steering.

stimuli: things that rouse the mind or spirit or incite to activity.

subjective: proceeding from or taking place in an individual's mind.

subordinate: of less importance; secondary.

summation: a work giving a summary of a whole subject.

tenets: principles or beliefs held as truths.

time track: the consecutive record of mental image pictures which accumulates through a person's life or lives. It is very exactly dated. The time track is the entire sequence of "now" incidents, complete with all perceptics, picked up by a person during his whole existence.

Tone Scale: a scale which shows the emotional tones of a person. These, ranged from the highest to the lowest, are, in part, serenity, enthusiasm (as we proceed downward), conservatism, boredom, antagonism, anger, covert hostility, fear, grief, apathy.

transcended: gone beyond the limits of; overstepped; exceeded.

traumatic: of or pertaining to a shocking or startling experience that has a lasting mental effect.

travail: intense pain; agony.

two-way communication: a normal cycle of a communication between two people. A two-way cycle of communication would work as follows: Joe, having originated a communication, and having completed it, may then wait for Bill to originate a communication to Joe, thus completing the remainder of the two-way cycle.

unrelenting: not easing or slackening in severity.

valences: personalities. Theoretically a person could have his own valence. But, more familiarly, the term is used to denote the borrowing of the personality of another. The word *valence* means, in Latin, "strength" *(valentia)*. We use it in Dianetics and Scientology as meaning personality, but it has not escaped the value of strength. A person takes at will the valences of a commanding nature or valences of a very obedient nature in order to answer up to various situations.

vantage point: position which allows a clear and broad view, understanding.

vilify: to use abusive or slanderous language about.

Voltaire, François: (1694–1778) French writer and philosopher.

Wundt, Wilhelm: (1832–1920) German physiologist and psychologist.

yearns: deeply longs or desires.

Index

Aberration,
  brought about by, 33
  cause and effect and, 94
  common denominator of, 77
  forced exteriorization and, 69–70
  games are aberrative, 115
  is basically a consideration, 87
  know, not-know and, 99
  prevention of, 108
ability,
  life and ability to create,
      uncreate and postulate, 60
  of preclear to have, not-know
      and play a game, 121
  of static, 83
  of thetan, 87
  to grant beingness, 28
  to play a game, 60
action, *see also* **cycle of action**
  defined, 18
  dictated by reactive mind, 68
actual, defined, 19
actual cycle of action, 20; *see also*
    cycle of action
  defined, 19
affinity, *see also* **ARC; ARC**
    triangle; communication;
    reality
  defined, 45–46
  relationship to communication
      and reality, 46–47

agreement, 46; *see also* **reality**
alcohol, 121
analytical mind, *see also* **mind;**
    thetan
  description of, 67
  somatic mind and, 70–71
anchor points, defined, 73
anesthetics, 68–69
animal, man as an, 9–10
animal dynamic, 40; *see also*
    dynamics
anxiety,
  caused by, 89
  prevailing, 90
  to be an effect, 91
apparency, *see also* **cycle of action**
  defined, 18
  of survival and cycle of action,
      20
  of time, 84
  reality and, 21
ARC, 46–48; *see also* **affinity; ARC**
    triangle; communication;
    reality
ARC triangle, 45–48; *see also*
    affinity; ARC;
    communication; reality
  as tool in human relationships,
      46–48
  defined, 45–47

exteriorization, *see also* **thetan**
aberrative type, 69–70
as goal of processing, 65
from mind, 69–70
handling of preclear and, 124
facsimile, *see also* **mind**
defined, 66
energy of, 71–72
failure,
executive, 53
fear of, 127
in government and business, 53
fixation, 32–33
forgetting, 124
Frederick of Prussia, 93–94
freedom, *see also* **game**
among barriers, 52–53
anatomy of games and, 128
balance of barriers and, 52–53, 54
effect of endless freedom, 52–56
in absence of barriers, 53
problems and, 35–36
pursuit of, 59–60
war cry of, 55–56
freedom from, 53
French Revolution, 55–56
future,
not-knowing, 100, 123
of Scientology, 133–134
responsibility for, 75–76
game, *see also* **barriers; freedom; purpose**
ability of preclear to play, 120–121, 124–125
ability to play consists of, 60
anatomy of, and havingness, not-know, purposes, freedom, 128
are aberrative, 115–116
being forced to play, 60
conditions of existence and game of life, 28
defined, 51, 52, 56, 116
elements of, 52–53, 59–60
everyone is engaged in several games, 54

game, *(cont.)*
exterior view of, 52
goal of Scientology and, 103
havingness and, 34–35, 124–125
invention of, 124–125
life understood as a, 51–52
no-effect and, 89
pan-determinism or self-determinism and, 54–56
problems and, 125
repeated failure in, 89
scarcity of, 116, 125
type determined by, 116
universes considered in, 85–86
willing to win or lose, 127
game conditions, 116–117; *see also* **game; no-game conditions**
Genghis Khan, 93–94
glandular system, 70–71
God dynamic, 40–41; *see also* **dynamics**
good manager, 56–57
government, 3–4, 53
gradient scale, defined, 119–120
Gray's Anatomy, 72
group dynamic, 40; *see also* **dynamics**
H-bomb, 4–5
hallucination, defined, 66
happiness, 56–57
have,
ability of preclear to have, not-know and play a game, 121
effect and, 35
havingness, *see also* **beingness; doingness**
anatomy of games and, 128
counter-position to, 128
defined, 27–28
game and, 34–35, 124–125
reduction of, in session, 131
remedy for deterioration of, 123
heaven, 5

Books and Tapes
by L. Ron Hubbard

To obtain any of the following materials by L. Ron Hubbard, contact the organization nearest you, or order directly from the publisher. These addresses are given at the very back of this publication. Many of these works have been translated and are available in a number of different languages.

The works are arranged in the suggested order that they be read (or listened to) within each category.

Basic Scientology Books

A New Slant on Life • Have you ever asked yourself Who am I? What am I? This book of articles by L. Ron Hubbard answers these all too common questions. This is knowledge one can use every day—for a new, more confident and happier slant on life!

The Problems of Work • Work plays a big part in the game of life. Do you really enjoy your work? Are you certain of your job security? Would you like the increased personal satisfaction of doing your work well? This is the book that shows exactly how to achieve these things and more. The game of life—and within it, the game of work—can be enjoyable and rewarding.

Scientology 0-8: The Book of Basics • What is life? Did you know an individual can create space, energy and time? Here are the basics of life itself, and the secrets of becoming cause over any area of your life. Discover how you can use the data in this book to achieve your goals.

Basic Dianetics Books

Dianetics: The Modern Science of Mental Health • Acclaimed as the most effective self-help book ever published. Dianetics technology has helped millions reach new heights of freedom and ability. Over 11,000,000 copies sold! Discover the source of mental barriers that prevent you from achieving your goals—and how to handle them!

Self Analysis • The complete do-it-yourself handbook for anyone who wants to improve his abilities and success potential. Use the simple, easy-to-learn techniques in *Self Analysis* to build self-confidence and reduce stress.

The Dynamics of Life—An Introduction to Dianetics Discoveries • Break through the barriers to your happiness. In this book, L. Ron Hubbard reveals the startling principles behind Dianetics—facts so powerful they can change forever the way you look at yourself and your potentials. Discover how you can use the powerful basic principles in this book to blast through the barriers of your mind and gain full control over your success, future and happiness.

Dianetics: The Evolution of a Science • It is estimated that we use less than ten percent of our mind's potential. What stops us from developing and using the full potential of our minds? *Dianetics: The Evolution of a Science* is L. Ron Hubbard's incredible story of how he discovered the reactive mind and how he developed the keys to unlock its secrets. Get this firsthand account of what the mind really is, and how you can release its hidden potential.

Books on the Purification Program

Purification: An Illustrated Answer to Drugs • Do toxins and drugs hold down your ability to think clearly? What is the Purification Program and how does it work? How can harmful chemical substances be gotten out of the body? Our society is ridden by abuse of drugs, alcohol and medicine that reduce one's ability to think clearly. Find out what can be done in this introduction to the Purification Program.

All About Radiation • Can the effects of radiation exposure be avoided or reduced? What exactly would happen in the event of an atomic explosion? Get the answers to these and many other questions in this illuminating book. *All About Radiation* describes observations and discoveries concerning the physical and mental effects of radiation and the possibilities for handling them. Get the real facts on the subject of radiation and its effects.

Books on Past Lives

Have You Lived Before This Life? • This is the book that sparked a flood of interest in the ancient puzzle: Does man live only one life? The answer lay in mystery, buried until L. Ron Hubbard's researches unearthed the truth. Actual case histories of people recalling past lives in auditing tell the tale.

Mission Into Time • Here is a fascinating account of a unique research expedition into both space and time, locating physical evidence of past lives in an area rich with history—the Mediterranean.

Dianetics Graduate Books

Science of Survival • If you ever wondered why people act the way they do, you'll find this book a wealth of information. It's vital to anyone who wants to understand others and improve personal relationships. *Science of Survival* is built around a remarkable chart—The Hubbard Chart of Human Evaluation. With it you can understand and predict other people's behavior and reactions and greatly increase your control over your own life. This is a valuable handbook that can make a difference between success and failure on the job and in life.

Dianetics 55! • Your success in life depends on your ability to communicate. Do you know a formula exists for communication? Learn the rules of better communication that can help you live a more fulfilling life. Here, L. Ron Hubbard deals with the fundamental principles of communication and how you can master these to achieve your goals.

Child Dianetics • Here is a revolutionary new approach to raising children with the techniques of Dianetics technology. Find out how you can help your child achieve greater confidence, more self-reliance, improved learning rate and a happier, more loving relationship with you.

Notes on the Lectures • In the rush of excitement following the release of *Dianetics: The Modern Science of Mental Health*, L. Ron Hubbard was in demand all over the world as a speaker. This book is compiled from his fascinating lectures given right after the publication of *Dianetics: The Modern Science of Mental Health*. In them, he expands on the powerful principles of Dianetics and its application to groups.

The Advanced Scientology Library

Scientology 8-8008 • Get the basic truths about your nature as a spiritual being and your relationship to the physical universe around you. Here, L. Ron Hubbard describes procedures designed to increase your abilities to heights previously only dreamed of.

Scientology 8-80 • What are the laws of life? We are all familiar with physical laws such as the law of gravity, but what laws govern life and thought? L. Ron Hubbard answers the riddles of life and its goals in the physical universe.

Scientology: A History of Man • A fascinating look at the history of the human race—revolutionary concepts guaranteed to intrigue you and challenge many basic assumptions about man's true power, potential and abilities.

The Phoenix Lectures • An in-depth look at the roots of Scientology religious philosophy and how it was developed is contained in this work. The influence of earlier great philosophies and religious leaders is covered in detail. This is followed by a complete discussion of the nature of existence and reality, and exactly how man interacts with his environment. An enlightening look at the infinite potentialities of man.

The Creation of Human Ability • Improve your life, and the lives of others, far beyond current expectations. Learn simple yet powerful techniques you can use to help somebody increase his ability and operate more successfully in life.

Handbook for Preclears • This personal workbook contains easily done exercises to help you improve your life and find greater happiness.

Advanced Procedure and Axioms • For the *first* time the basics of thought and the physical universe have been codified into a set of fundamental laws, signaling an entire new way to view and approach the subjects of man, the physical universe and even life itself.

Dictionaries

Basic Dictionary of Dianetics and Scientology • Compiled from the works of L. Ron Hubbard, this convenient dictionary contains the terms and expressions needed by anyone learning Dianetics and Scientology technology. And a *special bonus*—an easy-to-read Scientology Organizing Board chart that shows you whom to contact for services and information at your nearest Scientology Organization.

Dianetics and Scientology Technical Dictionary • This dictionary is your indispensable guide to the words and ideas of Scientology and Dianetics technologies—technologies which can help you increase your know-how and effectiveness in life. Over three thousand words are defined—including a new understanding of vital words like *life, love* and *happiness* as well as Scientology terms.

Modern Management Technology Defined: Hubbard Dictionary of Administration and Management • Here's a real breakthrough in the subject of administration and management! Eighty-six hundred words are defined for greater understanding of any business situation. Clear, precise Scientology definitions describe many previously baffling phenomena and bring truth, sanity and understanding to the often murky field of business management.

Basic Executive Books

How to Live Though an Executive • What is the one factor in business and commerce which, if lacking, can keep a person overworked and worried, keep labor and management at each other's throats, and make an unsafe working atmosphere? L. Ron Hubbard reveals principles based on years of research into many different types of organizations.

Introduction to Scientology Ethics • Find out how to improve conditions and reach higher states of awareness and survival in one's job, family and life. Here's a practical book to be applied in all aspects of your life. *Introduction to Scientology Ethics* explains how to live a more honest and ethical life. Here is a practical system for helping you achieve your goals.

Graduate Executive Books

Organization Executive Course • The *Organization Executive Course* volumes contain workable organizational technology never before known to man. This is not just how a Scientology organization works; this is how the operation of *any* organization, *any* activity, can be improved. A person knowing the data in these volumes fully, and applying it, could completely reverse any downtrend in a company—or even a country!

Management Series Volume 1 • Never before has such a collection of state-of-the-art management technology been available for instant use. This large volume gives you the secrets of organizing anything to flow smoothly and efficiently with increased production and viability.

Management Series Volume 2 • Here is high-tech for any business executive or manager. In this 768-page volume you get down to the basics of finance, personnel, marketing and public relations. Get powerful data to strategically plan and coordinate so you can accomplish any objective. Learn how to be a powerful, effective executive and stay one.

Reference Materials

Background and Ceremonies of the Church of Scientology • Discover the beautiful and inspiring ceremonies of the Church of Scientology, and its fascinating religious and historical background. This book contains the illuminating Creed of the

Church, church services, sermons and ceremonies, many as originally given in person by L. Ron Hubbard, Founder of Scientology.

What is Scientology? • Scientology applied religious philosophy has attracted great interest and attention since its beginning. What is Scientology philosophy? What can it accomplish —and why are so many people from all walks of life proclaiming its effectiveness? Find the answers to these questions and many others in *What is Scientology?*

Books to Help You Counsel Others

Introductory and Demonstration Processes and Assists • How can you help someone increase his enthusiasm for living? How can you improve someone's self-confidence on the job? Here are basic Scientology processes you can use to help others deal with life and living.

Volunteer Minister's Handbook • This is a big, practical how-to-do-it book to give a person the basic knowledge on how to help self and others through the rough spots in life. It consists of twenty-one sections—each one covering important situations in life, such as drug and alcohol problems, study difficulties, broken marriages, accidents and illnesses, failing businesses, difficult children, and much more. This is the basic tool with which to help someone out of troubles, and bring about a happier life.

The Classic Cassettes Series

There are nearly three thousand recorded lectures by L. Ron Hubbard on the subjects of Dianetics and Scientology. What follows is a sampling of these lectures, each known and loved the world over. All of the Classic Cassettes are presented in Clearsound state-of-the-art sound-recording technology, notable for its clarity and brilliance of reproduction.

Scientology and Effective Knowledge • Voyage to new horizons of awareness! *Scientology and Effective Knowledge* by L. Ron Hubbard can help you understand more about yourself and others. A fascinating tale of the beginnings of Dianetics and Scientology.

The Story of Dianetics and Scientology • In this lecture, L. Ron Hubbard shares with you his earliest insights into human nature and gives a compelling and often humorous account of his experiences. Spend an unforgettable time with Ron as he talks about the start of Dianetics and Scientology!

The Road to Truth • The road to truth has eluded man since the beginning of time. In this classic lecture, L. Ron Hubbard explains what this road actually is and why it is the only road one MUST travel all the way once begun. This lecture reveals the only road to higher levels of living.

My Philosophy • Three dramatic essays by Ron—"My Philosophy," "The Aims of Scientology" and "A Description of Scientology"—come alive for you in this cassette. These powerful writings, beautifully read and set to new and inspiring music, tell you what Scientology is, what it does and what its aims are.

More advanced books and lectures are available. Contact your nearest organization or write directly to the publisher for a full catalog.

"The success level of a person *is* his communication level."

—*L. Ron Hubbard*

Your success on the job, in handling a home, in creating relationships based on *honesty* and *trust* depends on *your ability to communicate.*

The Success Through Communication Course by L. Ron Hubbard is a vital and *practical* course to help you improve communication and be more effective in life. Discover the eighteen exact, simple and powerful techniques that will show you how to:

- Get your point across, and really be understood!

- Begin a conversation with anyone—even with a silent person!

- Listen effectively!

- Handle any upset in communication!

- End any conversation when you want to

  —and much more!

Learn these effective communication techniques on weekdays, evenings or weekends.

Do the *Success Through Communication Course* by L. Ron Hubbard

Start today!

Improve Your Life
with Scientology
Extension Courses

Scientology books by L. Ron Hubbard give you the knowledge to achieve a happier, more successful life. Now learn to take and *use* that knowledge to gain greater control of *your* life. Enroll on a Scientology Extension Course.

Each extension course package includes a lesson booklet with easy to understand instructions and all the lessons you will need to complete it. Each course can be done in the comfort and convenience of your own home. Simply mail the completed lessons once a week to the Extension Course Supervisor at your Church of Scientology, who will review it and mail the results back to you. When you complete the course you will be sent a beautiful certificate suitable for framing.

The Fundamentals of Thought
Extension Course

Here is *practical, workable* knowledge that can improve your life in today's troubled world. The *Fundamentals of Thought Extension Course* contains lessons to ensure that you fully understand the data and can use it. Under the guidance of a professional Extension Course Supervisor, you can gain far greater understanding of life as you complete each lesson by mail. Order the *Fundamentals of Thought Extension Course* today!

A New Slant on Life
Extension Course

Life does not have to remain the same. You *can* reach higher levels of knowledge, ability and freedom. Discover the two rules for happy living, the secret of success, how to avoid being a "cog in a machine," how to reach your goals and more. Do the *New Slant on Life Extension Course* and gain a refreshing new outlook on life!

The Problems of Work
Extension Course

Trying to handle a job and keep it can get to be a deadlier struggle with each working day. What are the secrets to increasing your enjoyment of work? How can you gain the personal satisfaction of doing your work well? Find the answers and apply them easily. Do *The Problems of Work Extension Course!*

Enroll on a
Scientology Home Study
Extension Course Today!

For information and enrollment and prices for these Extension Courses and the books they accompany, contact the Public Registrar at your nearest Church of Scientology. (A complete list of Scientology Churches and Organizations is provided at the back of this book.)

Get Your Free Catalog of Knowledge on How to Improve Life

L. Ron Hubbard's books and tapes increase your ability to understand yourself and others. His works give you the practical know-how you need to improve your life and the lives of your family and friends.

Many more materials by L. Ron Hubbard are available than have been covered in the pages of this book. A free catalog of these materials is available on request.

Write for your free catalog today!

Bridge Publications, Inc.
4571 Fountain Avenue
Los Angeles, California 90029

"I am always happy to hear from my readers."

L. Ron Hubbard

These were the words of L. Ron Hubbard, who was always very interested in hearing from his friends, readers and followers. He made a point of staying in communication with everyone he came in contact with over his fifty-year career as a professional writer, and he had thousands of fans and friends that he corresponded with all over the world.

The publishers of L. Ron Hubbard's literary works wish to continue this tradition and would welcome letters and comments from you, his readers, both old and new.

Any message addressed to the Author's Affairs Director at Bridge Publications will be given prompt and full attention.

Bridge Publications, Inc.
4751 Fountain Avenue
Los Angeles, California 90029
U.S.A.

Church and Organization
Address List

Albuquerque
Church of Scientology
1210 San Pedro NE
Albuquerque, New Mexico 87110

Ann Arbor
Church of Scientology
301 North Ingalls Street
Ann Arbor, Michigan 48104

Austin
Church of Scientology
2200 Guadalupe
Austin, Texas 78705

Boston
Church of Scientology
448 Beacon Street
Boston, Massachusetts 02115-1099

Buffalo
Church of Scientology
47 West Huron Street
Buffalo, New York 14202

Chicago
Church of Scientology
3011 North Lincoln Avenue
Chicago, Illinois 60657

Cincinnati
Church of Scientology
215 West 4th Street, 5th Floor
Cincinnati, Ohio 45202-2625

Columbus
Church of Scientology
167 East State Street
Columbus, Ohio 43215

Dallas
Church of Scientology
Celebrity Centre Dallas
8501 Manderville Lane
Dallas, Texas 75231

Denver
Church of Scientology
375 South Navajo Street
Denver, Colorado 80223

Detroit
Church of Scientology
321 Williams Street
Royal Oak, Michigan 48067

Honolulu
Church of Scientology
1100 Alakea Street #301
Honolulu, Hawaii 96813

Kansas City
Church of Scientology
3742 Broadway, Suite 203
Kansas City, Missouri 64111

Las Vegas
Church of Scientology
846 East Sahara Avenue
Las Vegas, Nevada 89104

Las Vegas *(cont.)*
Church of Scientology
Celebrity Centre Las Vegas
1100 South 10th Street
Las Vegas, Nevada 89104-1505

Long Island
Church of Scientology
330 Fulton Avenue
Hempstead, New York 11550

Los Angeles and vicinity
Church of Scientology
4810 Sunset Boulevard
Los Angeles, California 90027

Church of Scientology
1451 Irvine Boulevard
Tustin, California 92680

Church of Scientology
263 East Colorado Boulevard
Pasadena, California 91101

Church of Scientology
10335 Magnolia Boulevard
North Hollywood, California 91601

Church of Scientology
American Saint Hill Organization
1413 North Berendo Street
Los Angeles, California 90027

Church of Scientology
American Saint Hill Foundation
1413 North Berendo Street
Los Angeles, California 90027

Church of Scientology
Advanced Organization of
  Los Angeles
1306 North Berendo Street
Los Angeles, California 90027

Church of Scientology
Celebrity Centre International
5930 Franklin Avenue
Hollywood, California 90028

Miami
Church of Scientology
120 Giralda Avenue
Coral Gables, Florida 33134

Minneapolis
Church of Scientology
3019 Minnehaha Avenue
Minneapolis, Minnesota 55406-1931

New Haven
Church of Scientology
909 Whalley Avenue
New Haven, Connecticut 06515

New York City
Church of Scientology
227 West 46th Street
New York City, New York 10036

Church of Scientology
Celebrity Centre New York
65 East 82nd Street
New York City, New York 10028

Orlando
Church of Scientology
710-A East Colonial Drive
Orlando, Florida 32803

Philadelphia
Church of Scientology
1315 Race Street
Philadelphia, Pennsylvania 19107

Phoenix
Church of Scientology
4450 North Central Avenue, Suite 102
Phoenix, Arizona 85012

Portland
Church of Scientology
1536 South East 11th Avenue
Portland, Oregon 97214

Church of Scientology
Celebrity Centre Portland
709 South West Salmon Street
Portland, Oregon 97205

Sacramento
Church of Scientology
825 15th Street
Sacramento, California 95814-2096

San Diego
Church of Scientology
2409 Fourth Avenue
San Diego, California 92101

San Francisco
Church of Scientology
83 McAllister Street
San Francisco, California 94102

San Jose
Church of Scientology
3604 Stevens Creek Boulevard
San Jose, California 95117

Santa Barbara
Church of Scientology
524 State Street
Santa Barbara, California 93101

Seattle
Church of Scientology
2004 Westlake Avenue
Seattle, Washington 98121

St. Louis
Church of Scientology
9510 Page Boulevard
St. Louis, Missouri 63132

Tampa
Church of Scientology
4809 North Armenia Avenue, Suite 215
Tampa, Florida 33603

Clearwater
Church of Scientology
Flag® Service Organization
210 South Fort Harrison Avenue
Clearwater, Florida 33516

Washington, D.C.
Founding Church of Scientology
2125 "S" Street N.W.
Washington, D.C. 20008

Canada

Edmonton
Church of Scientology
10349 82nd Avenue
Edmonton, Alberta
Canada T6E 1Z9

Kitchener
Church of Scientology
8 Water Street North
Kitchener, Ontario
Canada N2H 5A5

Montreal
Church of Scientology
4489 Papineau Street
Montréal, Québec
Canada H2H 1T7

Ottawa
Church of Scientology
150 Rideau Street, 2nd Floor
Ottawa, Ontario
Canada K1N 5X6

Quebec
Church of Scientology
226 St-Joseph est
Québec, Québec
Canada G1K 3A9

Toronto
Church of Scientology
696 Yonge Street
Toronto, Ontario
Canada M4Y 2A7

Vancouver
Church of Scientology
401 West Hastings Street
Vancouver, British Columbia
Canada V6B 1L5

Winnipeg
Church of Scientology
Suite 125—388 Donald Street
Winnipeg, Manitoba
Canada R3B 2J4

United Kingdom

Birmingham
Church of Scientology
80 Hurst Street
Birmingham
England B5 4TD

Brighton
Church of Scientology
Dukes Arcade, Top Floor
Dukes Street
Brighton, Sussex
England

East Grinstead
Saint Hill Foundation
Saint Hill Manor
East Grinstead, West Sussex
England RH19 4JY

Advanced Organization Saint Hill
Saint Hill Manor
East Grinstead, West Sussex
England RH19 4JY

Edinburgh
Hubbard Academy of Personal
   Independence
20 Southbridge
Edinburgh, Scotland EH1 1LL

London
Church of Scientology
68 Tottenham Court Road
London, W1P 0BB England

Manchester
Church of Scientology
258 Deansgate
Manchester, England M3 4BG

Plymouth
Church of Scientology
41 Ebrington Street
Plymouth, Devon
England PL4 9AA

Sunderland
Church of Scientology
51 Fawcett Street
Sunderland, Tyne and Wear
England SR1 1RS

Austria

Vienna
Church of Scientology
Mariahilfer Strasse 88A/II/2
A-1070 Vienna, Austria

Belgium

Brussels
Church of Scientology
45A, Rue de l'Ecuyer
1000 Bruxelles, Belgium

Denmark

Aarhus
Church of Scientology
Guldsmedegade 17, 2
8000 Aarhus C, Denmark

Copenhagen
Church of Scientology
Store Kongensgade 55
1264 Copenhagen K, Denmark

Church of Scientology
Vesterbrogade 23 A – 25
1620 Copenhagen V, Denmark

Church of Scientology
Advanced Organization Saint Hill for
   Europe and Africa
Jernbanegade 6
1608 Copenhagen V, Denmark

France

Angers
Church of Scientology
10–12, rue Max Richard
49000 Angers, France

Clermont-Ferrand
Church of Scientology
2 Pte Rue Giscard de la Tour Fondue
63000 Clermont-Ferrand, France

Lyon
Church of Scientology
3, place des Capucins
69001 Lyon, France

Paris
Church of Scientology
65, rue de Dunkerque
75009 Paris, France

Church of Scientology
Celebrity Centre Paris
69, rue Legendre
75017 Paris, France

St. Etienne
Church of Scientology
24, rue Marengo
42000 St. Etienne, France

Germany

Berlin
Church of Scientology e.V.
Sponholzstrasse 51/52
1000 Berlin 41, Germany

Düsseldorf
Church of Scientology
Friedrichstrasse 28
4000 Düsseldorf, West Germany

Frankfurt
Church of Scientology
Darmstadter Landstr. 119–125
6000 Frankfurt/Main, West Germany

Hamburg
Church of Scientology e.V.
Steindamm 63
2000 Hamburg 1, West Germany

Church of Scientology
Celebrity Centre Hamburg
Mönckebergstrasse 5
2000 Hamburg 1
West Germany

Munich
Church of Scientology e.V.
Beichstrasse 12
D-8000 München 40, West Germany

Greece

Athens
Applied Philosophy Center of Greece
   (K.E.F.E.)
Ippokratous 175B
114 72 Athens, Greece

Israel

Tel Aviv
Scientology and Dianetics College
7 Salomon Street
Tel Aviv 66023, Israel

Italy

Brescia
Church of Scientology
Dei Tre Laghi
Via Fratelli Bronzetti N. 20
25125 Brescia, Italy

Milano
Church of Scientology
Via Abetone, 10
20137 Milano, Italy

Monza
Church of Scientology
Via Cavour, 5
20052 Monza, Italy

Novara
Church of Scientology
Corso Cavallotti No. 7
28100 Novara, Italy

Nuoro
Church of Scientology
Corso Garibaldi, 108
08100 Nuoro, Italy

Padua
Church of Scientology
Via Mameli 1/5
35131 Padova, Italy

Pordenone
Church of Scientology
Via Montereale, 10/C
33170 Pordenone, Italy

Rome
Church of Scientology
Via di San Vito, 11
00185 Roma, Italy

Turin
Church of Scientology
Via Guarini, 4
10121 Torino, Italy

Verona
Church of Scientology
Vicolo Chiodo No. 4/A
37121 Verona, Italy

Netherlands

Amsterdam
Church of Scientology
Nieuwe Zijds Voorburgwal 271
1012 RL Amsterdam, Netherlands

Norway

Oslo
Church of Scientology
Storgata 9
0155 Oslo 1, Norway

Portugal

Lisbon
Instituto de Dianética
Rua Actor Taborde 39–4°
1000 Lisboa, Portugal

Spain

Barcelona
Dianética
Calle Pau Claris 85, Principal 1ª
08010 Barcelona, Spain

Madrid
Asociación Civil de Dianética
Montera 20, Piso 2
28013 Madrid, Spain

Sweden

Göteborg
Church of Scientology
Norra Hamngatan 4
S-411 14 Göteborg, Sweden

Malmö
Church of Scientology
Stortorget 27
S-211 34 Malmö, Sweden

Stockholm
Church of Scientology
Kammakargatan 46
S-111 60 Stockholm, Sweden

Switzerland

Basel
Church of Scientology
Herrengrabenweg 56
4054 Basel, Switzerland

Bern
Church of Scientology
Effingerstrasse 25
CH-3008 Bern, Switzerland

Geneva
Church of Scientology
4, rue du Léman
1201 Genève, Switzerland

Lausanne
Church of Scientology
10, rue de la Madeleine
1003 Lausanne, Switzerland

Zurich
Church of Scientology
Badenerstrasse 294
CH-8004 Zürich, Switzerland

Australia

Adelaide
Church of Scientology
24 Waymouth Street
Adelaide, South Australia 5000
Australia

Brisbane
Church of Scientology
106 Edward Street, 2nd Floor
Brisbane, Queensland 4000
Australia

Canberra
Church of Scientology
108 Bunda Street, Suite 16
Canberra Civic
A.C.T. 2601, Australia

Melbourne
Church of Scientology
44 Russell Street
Melbourne, Victoria 3000
Australia

Perth
Church of Scientology
39–41 King Street
Perth, Western Australia 6000
Australia

Sydney
Church of Scientology
201 Castlereagh Street
Sydney, New South Wales 2000
Australia

Church of Scientology
Advanced Organization Saint Hill
    Australia, New Zealand and
    Oceania
19–37 Greek Street
Glebe, New South Wales 2037
Australia

Japan

Tokyo
Scientology Organization
101 Toyomi Nishi Gotanda Heights
2-13-5 Nishi Gotanda
Shinagawa-Ku
Tokyo, Japan 141

New Zealand

Auckland
Church of Scientology
44 Queen Street, 2nd Floor
Auckland 1, New Zealand

Africa

Bulawayo
Church of Scientology
74 Abercorn Street
Bulawayo, Zimbabwe